HUMBLEBRAG

HUMBLEBRAG

The Art of False Modesty

HARRIS WITTELS

GRAND CENTRAL
PUBLISHING

NEW YORK   BOSTON

Grand Central Publishing
Hachette Book Group
237 Park Avenue
New York, NY 10017

www.HachetteBookGroup.com

Printed in the United States of America

RRD-C

First Edition: September 2012
10 9 8 7 6 5 4 3 2 1

Grand Central Publishing is a division of Hachette Book Group, Inc.
The Grand Central Publishing name and logo is a trademark of Hachette Book Group, Inc.

The Hachette Speakers Bureau provides a wide range of authors for speaking events. To find out more, go to www.hachettespeakersbureau.com or call (866) 376-6591.

The publisher is not responsible for websites (or their content) that are not owned by the publisher.

Library of Congress Cataloging-in-Publication Data
Wittels, Harris.
    Humblebrag : the art of false modesty / Harris Wittels. —1st ed.
        p. cm.
    ISBN 978-1-455-51418-2
    1. Quotations, English.   2. Wit and humor.   3. Twitter.   4. Social media.
I. Title.
    PN6084.H8W65 2012
    082—dc23
                                                                    2012016126

Dedicated to
Mom, Dad, Steph, Ganny, and Scarlett Johansson

Contents

Author's Note

If you were included in this book, while I can see how you would think I'm a dick, I hope that you know it's all in good fun. Everyone humblebrags. I do it too. A lot. Thanks for being a chiller.

Introduction

Man, I can't believe this dumb little word I came up with actually got me a book deal.

Did that last sentence annoy you? It should have. But, can you not quite put your finger on *why* it annoyed you? Well, it's because that type of statement is what I like to call a "humblebrag" and it's what this book is all about. First, let's define a humblebrag.

humblebrag (huhm-buhl'brag)
noun, verb

1. a specific type of brag that masks the boasting part of a statement in a faux-humble guise. The false humility allows the offender to boast about their "achievements" without any sense of shame or guilt. Humblebrags are usually self-deprecating in nature, but there are a few exceptions, which are mentioned later in the book.

Here is an example of a standard humblebrag, which was tweeted by late-night talk show host, Craig Ferguson, aka @CraigyFerg: **"I just got nominated for a damn Grammy. Take that low self esteem. #fuckyeah."** The brag element of his tweet is that he was nominated for a Grammy, whereas the humble element is his low self-esteem. Here is another example from some fellow named Sam Halliday (@samhallidayTDCC) from some band called Two Door Cinema Club: **"Our song has just come on the radio in our taxi. Awkward!"** In this tweet, he is bragging about his band's song being played on the radio, while disguising it as an "awkward" situation that he was forced to endure. (Incidentally, the use of the words "awkward" or "weird" are quite commonly used in humblebrags. In fact, there is a whole section of the book devoted to it. Don't skip to it. Just take my word for it for now.)

Hopefully, you're getting the hang of it now. It's not difficult. This book is basically a collection of my favorite humblebrags I've found on Twitter and elsewhere. Also there are some jokes about said humblebrags, and then also some other stuff. I hope you enjoy it; it was really a pain in the ass to write. (See? That was another humblebrag.)

I didn't really notice humblebrags until I moved to Los Angeles in 2006. I love living here, but, man—going to a party out here is a nonstop humblebrag-fest; people complaining about how their pilots probably won't get picked up or how a studio gave their screenplay some shitty notes. It can be truly endless. It's just kinda how people communicate out here. I am generalizing, of course. Not everyone in LA does that. Also, it isn't just in LA that people are shamelessly self-promotional/aggrandizing. I am sure that, right now, somewhere in Brooklyn, a street artist is saying he put a picture of Mao Tse-tung on the highest Nike billboard, but it sucks that he got arrested. Or that in Ireland someone is saying he grew the biggest potato, but "Aye, was it hard work." It happens everywhere all the time, but I just noticed it in LA specifically. Yet, for a while, I couldn't name exactly what I was noticing. I just knew it wasn't straight-up bragging.

Then, Twitter blew up and I started constantly seeing these kinds of statements typed out for the world to see. This was the perfect medium for "it" and I finally identified what "it" was and why it annoyed me. It was bragging, but it wasn't just bragging. It was a type of bragging that included some amount of fake modesty, which somehow made it acceptable to do.

Every time I would read one, I would think, "Why would that person say that? What is the point?" It can only serve to make people jealous of you and/or hate you. No one ever hears one and actually thinks you are cooler. But people do it because it's in their nature to prove to others how great their life is, or maybe they're actually just trying to prove it...to themselves? Shit's deep, yo! I fought the impulse many times to respond to all of these offenders on Twitter with "Why did you feel the need to tell the world that?" But I was scared to burn bridges. Instead, I just silently stewed in my resentment for a couple of years. Then, I became too fed up with seeing people repeatedly doing it, so I once tweeted, "Guys, if you're going to brag, don't be humble about it. Just brag."

And from that I coined the phrase "humblebrag" and started up an anonymous Twitter account (twitter.com/humblebrag) where I would retweet any flagrant humblebraggers.

The first humblebrag I ever retweeted was by Donald Glover (an actor on NBC's *Community* and rapper Childish Gambino). He (@mrdonaldglover) tweeted: **"Its an honor to be the 1st thing japanese men see after reading their porn on the subway."** Then there was an attached photo of a Gap ad featuring a photo of himself. Clearly, he just wanted to let us all know he was in a Gap ad. That's where it all began. Childish Gambino has since name-checked "humblebrag" in one of his songs, making this whole thing worth it. (Wait, was *this* a humblebrag? Probably.) Then, I retweeted a few more from a few different people, and a few more after that, and so on. Soon after, the Twitter account's follower count started to grow exponentially and people began emailing **humblebrag@gmail.com** with suggestions for people I could retweet—friends of theirs, bosses, celebrities they followed.

And what started as an inside joke between me and the writing staff at *Parks and Recreation* (where I work) became somewhat of a second job for me, where I would sift through hundreds of emails a week searching for leads on any humblebrags. It is most definitely a gigantic waste of time, but I like to think I am doing some sort of a service for society (#humblebrag)—putting humblebraggers in check, so that we can get back to a time when braggers either outright bragged like assholes or just didn't do it at all.

HUMBLEBRAG

Ugh, I Know Famous People!

Let's start off with one of the most commonly used form of humblebragging, which is the name-drop humblebrag. No one likes a name-dropper. Add to that some phony self-deprecation and you have a not fun thing. There are a couple kinds of these. One kind is committed by normal people and the other by celebrities. What's funny about normal people saying things like "I totally drank too much while hanging out with Johnny Depp" is that "hanging out" usually means they were at the same bar and drunkenly yelled at Johnny Depp that they went to the same high school. I bet Johnny Depp didn't consider it a hang. What's funny about when a celebrity does it is that it's usually an attempt to show that they're a normal person. They aren't though, is the thing.

Noah Harlan (@noahharlan)
In other news, Paul McCartney stole our golf cart. I'm serious. #HonoredOrPissed?

Paul McCartney, The Beatle, right? Soooo ... honored probably? Final answer.

Damon Lindelof (@DamonLindelof)
Sitting next to Penny Marshall at the Lakers Game.
#GEEKINGOUT

There is a chance he actually was geeking out there, but he's the creator of Lost. *He's been around famous people before. I have a slight bugaboo about celebrities trying to show that they are still normal and "on our level" by getting nervous around other celebrities.*

Josh Horowitz (@joshuahorowitz)
Dan Radcliffe just showed me a text he just got from JK
Rowling which just about blew my mind. Can't say what
it said. Sorry

Well, so why tell us this then, ya know? Also, I thought his name was Daniel, but I guess if you're close friends it's just "Dan" or something.

Kelly Bourdet (@kellybourdet)
Just spent 30 minutes on the phone with johnny knoxville
talking about period sex

K.

Machine Gun Kelly (@machinegunkelly)
You ever been called on stage by DMX in front of 20,000

people to perform a song and forgot the lyrics cuz u were
so nervous? I have lol

I'm going to go ahead and assume this was a rhetorical question.
He couldn't have possibly wondered if anyone besides himself has
forgotten DMX lyrics after being called up on stage, right? It's such
a specific and narrow margin of people who have experienced that.
That being said, if I were him I would have been more nervous to
tweet this than I would have to get on stage with DMX. Namely
because DMX hasn't been relevant in like, eight years and this tweet
was annoying (especially with the "lol" addition).

Also, his Twitter bio starts with "I like threesomes." Come on,
dude, let's try a little harder to not be a parody of a musician.

Wiz Khalifa (@RealWizKhalifa)
im very thankful that the isley brothers are lettin me
smoke wit them right now

That's beautiful, man.

actingkeith (@actingkeith)
OMG... getting two drunk movie stars home... to sleep...
is much rougher than getting one drunk movie star home
to sleep... #responsible

The only way this isn't a humblebrag is if actingkeith is a cab-
driver. Then it's just part of the job, and I respect his work ethic.

However, his Twitter name isn't "cabbingkeith"; it's "actingkeith," and thus, he is letting everyone know that he parties with "movie stars." Though, it kind of sounds like they just use him for rides.

🐑 🐑 🐑

Spike Lee (@SpikeLee)
Just Got Off Da Phone Wit' My Main Man MJ-Michael Jordan. He Was Laughing At Me Cuz' His BobCats Rolled Over Da Orange And Blue.Why?Why?Why?

This looks extremely hard to have typed—what with all the first-letter capping and non-English. Just knowing how much effort went into such a name-droppy statement makes this profoundly agitating. Hate to put you on blast, Spike, but you did the wrong *thing.*

🐑 🐑 🐑

Zachary Levi (@ZacharyLevi)
Just devoured a tray of oysters with @themandymoore & company. It's weird when you stop to think about what we eat.

We got a real "Spike Lee" over here! Come on, dude from Chuck, let's not get off topic here. Point is you were hanging with Mandy Moore. Fuck some oyster ponderings!

reggie watts (@reggiewatts)
Just had such a great conversation with JJ Abrams today.
Such an inspired ideaFactory he is. I regret only having
seen Cloverfield!#catchup

Well, hey man, some of us regret never having talked to J. J. Abrams.

Adam Shankman (@adammshankman)
Bonding with @eliroth over crying like a baby during
toystory 3, and resting for massive bday party tomorrow
night. Can't freakin wait

Adam Shankman is my number-one news source for Eli Roth conversation topics. I gotta say, though, I wonder if Eli knows that he just goes off and tweets what their conversations together were. If I were Eli (and I'm not), it would make talking to Adam Shankman way less fun.

brian redban (@redban)
So Thursday I met John Mayer, Friday I met 50 Cent.. at
this rate, tonight im smoking weed with Jim Morrison and
Terri Schiavo.

I don't truly get what this means. It has the cadence of a joke, but it really doesn't stack up on the back end, making sense-wise. Regardless: humblebrag.

Rex Sorgatz (@fimoculous)
Good or bad?: I recognize three or four acquaintances
every time I page through Lucky.

Bad.

Jeffrey Ross (@realjeffreyross)
Hey @JuddApatow What was that Quentin Tarantino
joke u told me while back? He's the honoree at our private
Friars Roast this Wednesday.

*The Boastmaster General! (What you need to know to understand
this brilliant play on words is that Jeff Ross refers to himself as the
"Roastmaster General.")*

Judalina Neira (@TheJudalina)
I have a meeting with a Coppola tomorrow and I
have absolutely no idea how I got it or what it's about.
(reality + tech something or other)

Alllllright, I'll bite: Which Coppola is it?

Judd Apatow (@JuddApatow)
Geek moment. Was introduced to Bono at a party. I said

my name clearly when introduced. Praying for any hint of Judd awareness. NOTHING.

As a writer who would like to have a movie made at some point, I probably will regret saying this, but I would maybe consider retiring the phrase "Judd awareness." (Also, Judd: Huge fan. Loved Freaks and Geeks, Undeclared, Superbad, *etc.)*

Kristen Ortiz (@LilMissKO)
In Hwood, when u take a pic w/a celeb, ur automatically dating them. 2 clear up NE rumors, I am NOT dating Zac Efron.My <3 is w/@samventura

No one suspected that. All good.

Nathan Barlowe (@bummerman)
I have written R&B, Country, Electro and now for Bon Jovi. Strange life indeed.

Writing music isn't that strange if you are a music writer. If Nathan Barlowe was a neurosurgeon who wrote for Bon Jovi, this might be kind of strange, but he isn't.

Chad Ochocinco (@ochocinco)
#justasking Does it mean I'm finally famous when Bill Clinton comes to my birthday party?

I think you were finally famous when you joined the NFL. You know that, right?

Mark Salling (@MarkSalling)
wow, was on the way to Clives party and had to turn around upon hearing the news. too tragic. God rest your soul Whitney.

A thing I see frequently in the humblebrag game is people taking someone's death and making it about themselves. I'm sure Mark was genuinely very sad about Whitney, but I don't think he needed to mention that he was on his way to "Clive's" party. Also, don't call him just "Clive." That's gross. Also, don't do it at all.

Michael Yo (@MichaelYo)
I hate taking pictures with @KimKardashian #Gorgeous…She makes me feel so ugly standing next to her :)..Not even going to tweet our photo.

She's prettier than you 'cause she's a girl.

James Cameron (@JimCameron)
ryan seacrest told me I had to get on Twitter. So here I am. First tweet. I feel younger already.

Titanic director droppin' the 'Crest!

Matt Braunger (@Braunger)
My second day of shooting with Bryan Cranston is almost over. I'm not bragging, I'm sad.

Hey hey hey, I'll be the judge of what you're doing!

Rachelle Lefevre (@RachelleLefevre)
Huge congrats 2 Paul Giamatti & Kevin Spacey on Globe noms! Worked w both on the films & they r beyond genius. Honored 2 have worked w them!

Sucks there's no Golden Globe for "making things about you."

Tina Cervasio (@MSGTina)
In @Amareisreal press conference and Kanye West just walked through and said hi to me and that just totally distracted me. #Knicks #msg

Sounds rough. Hopefully you could refocus. Thanks for sharing!

Billy Bush (@billybush)
Haha @jlo heard u just sent a bunch of Venus Goddess
razors to my office 4 me 2 give my wife…who needs 2
STOP using my razor on her legs!!

I, too, tweet all of my thank-you notes.

Dave Dameshek (@Dameshek)
Just was hangin on the field w Aniston, Sandler and
Owen Wilson, then yapped w Mel Blount. Yawn…

*I know this was intended as a joke, with the whole "yawn" thing,
but you are still genuinely conveying that information to us.*

David Hemingson (@DavidHemingson)
Just played tennis with Bradley Cooper, who has an arm
like a rocket. So: handsome, very cool and major athlete,
in case your keeping score.

We weren't keeping score.

karey dornetto (@kareydornetto)
chevy chase called me homophobic. #bestvdayever
Megan Ganz (@meganganz)

Chevy Chase asked if I was a lesbian. It was just like I always imagined it would be.

Dueling Chevy Chase brags!

Nathan Rabin (@nathanrabin)
I'm at a fancy hotel preparing to interview a famous rock star. My homeless chic look has never been more appropriate!

The ever impressive nameless name-drop. Nicely done, Rabin. Nicely done.

Brett Erlich (@bretterlich)
If you were wondering where Nick Lachey is, the answer is "this party I'm at."

No one has ever wondered that.

Lesley Kat (@lesleykat)
So um what does one wear to a party in which John Hamm is present?

I would say wear whatever's comfortable. He will not care one way or the other.

Derek Blasberg (@DerekBlasberg)
So I spill ONE drink at this party and of course the
ONE person to see it is @NicoleRichie, which means I'll
NEVER hear the end of it.

Wait, who won't you never hear the end of it from? Nicole Richie?
If so, why? Is that a thing of hers? Making fun of people for spilling
drinks? I don't get it.

Don Jamieson (@realdonjamieson)
Hanging with Kirk Hammett, Uli Jon Roth, Trunk,
Florentine at Soho House talking metal, drinking wine!
Not bad for a slob from NJ!

I can't stress this enough: Being in the same room as celebrities
doesn't qualify as "hanging out" with them.

DelbertShoopman (@DelbertShoopman)
Partying with Ashley Judd is overrated.
#thingsimdoingrightnow

You know how I know you aren't partying with Ashley Judd?
Because you're tweeting about partying with Ashley Judd.

Jason Pinter (@jasonpinter)
Pitchapalooza release calls me a 'local celebrity'.
Celebrities they approached first: the Naked Cowboy, the
Soup Nazi, Letterman's janitor.

Yeah, but what's Pitchapalooza . . . is the thing . . .

Greta Van Susteren (@gretawire)
Ugh. I just pocket dialed spokesperson for Pentagon.

*After I retweeted this one, Greta Van Susteren blogged about how
she didn't think this was a humblebrag because she calls the Pentagon
regularly for her job, so why would she brag about it?*

*Well, if you didn't think pocket dialing the spokesperson for the
Pentagon is interesting or unique, then why tweet about it at all?
Bam! Your move, Susteren!*

Matthew Lillard (@MatthewLillard)
Spirit awards today. Playing Mafia with Tim Tebow
tonight. Oscars tomorrow? Wtf!! I'm so cool this weekend.
Next week I'll be lame again.

*I love Matthew Lillard. Revelatory performances in Scream and
Serial Mom. Also, when I retweeted this tweet, he seemed genuinely*

embarrassed and I felt kinda bad. However, this is totally a Tebow-humblebrag. Also, sorry Matt, but playing Mafia with Tim Tebow is already pretty lame.

Tommy Johnagin (@tommyjohnagin)
i had a moment with tina fey tonight. then i lingered and ruined everything. typical.

You typically have moments with Tina Fey?

Charles Melton (@_MELTON_)
Hanging out with topher grace the other day wasn't that bad. Funny dude

That's good. Keep us posted.

Charles Thorp (@charlesthorp)
Talked about photography w/ Ryan Phillippe at the @Stoli party for Bang Bang Club (opens today). Apparently he's not any good at it either.

This was a suspenseful one. Thought it was gonna be all brag, but then he tacked on the humble right there at the end. Close one.

Jason Berger (@jayberger)
My email got hacked. So I just sent Olivia Munn an email
about Viagra. Great.

*Your Twitter got hacked. Someone is sending out tweets about how
Olivia Munn is in your email contacts.*

Fortune Feimster (@fortunefunny)
Just had a 30 minute conversation with John Mayer at the
SNL after party cuz he liked me on "Last Comic." How is
this my life?

*Yes, however in the world did you get John Mayer to talk to you?
Oh, wait, you are a girl and alive.*

Chris Brogan (@chrisbrogan)
In the odd department, was just emailing back and forth
with Jessica Biel's dad. Yeah.

Not that odd. Her dad isn't a famous actress. Nice try though.

Mancow Muller (@MancowMuller)
Drink w/ Bono @ Whiskey last night...SHOCKED he
remembered me.

Were you his bartender?

Andy Blanco (@andyblancomusic)
It's time for the Tonys! Watching them with the cast and
crew from two Tony nominated plays. I feel so much less
important right now.

For reals?? To me, you are so much MORE important right now.

Jamie Keiles (@msjamiekeiles)
still adjusting to being the kind of person who has met
people that are in the movies on her netflix queue.

*It ain't easy. Also, sidenote, every movie on the planet is on Netflix.
My home movies from childhood are on there. Point being, to meet
someone who is in a movie on Netflix ain't that special.*

David Rosiak (@DavidRosiak)
My day: hung out with Corey Feldman, spoke on a panel
and received a machete engraved with mine and Matt's
names. I have a strange life.

*Hanging out with Corey Feldman doesn't really deserve bragging rights
(sorry, Corey, it doesn't), but this guy is still bragging about it. It's like
an old philosophical question: If a brag isn't a brag, is it still a brag?*

Audrie Renee Segura (@Audrie_Segura)
So funny I'm always around celebrities half the time I
don't know who they are-i had a convo w/ Collin Farrel &
had no idea

Not that funny.

Melissa Tan (@melissatan)
Marshall from HIMYM tried to buy me a drink at Hemlock
last night, but it made me feel like he was cheating on
Lily! #IwatchtoomuchTV

I bet the actual story is that he successfully bought you a drink. Otherwise, you're an insane person who thinks TV is real?

Kaitlin Shram (@KaitlinHeather)
Just heard "goodbye my lover" by james blunt and had a
flashback 2 when he asked me to come to winnipeg with
him. #yikes

Man, sorry to hear about your Vietnam-level flashbacks. I don't know how you find the strength to carry on.

Elena Parasco (@Elepara)
hm. dancing with david beckham last night - overrated.
hes not that hot. and he dances to techno weird.

Thanks for the reconnaissance!

Jenny Mollen (@jennyandteets)
Help! I'm w Cory Feldman and I don't know how not to tell
him I loved THE BURBS!

*You are handling this situation very well! Also, this is the second
Corey Feldman humblebrag in the book. I think this is the most
work he's gotten in years.*

Kenna Burima (@KennaBurima)
You know yer exhausted when you meet Dallas Green in
the lobby and he invites you for a drink but you opt for
the heavenly bed instead #cfmf

*This is like a shitty, humblebrag version of a Jeff Foxworthy "You
might be a redneck if..." joke.*

Ugh, Flying First Class Is So Ugh!

I have never seen someone fly first class without telling someone about it. I get it. It's exciting, but NO ONE wants to hear about it. It either means you are rich or got upgraded due to your mileage reward points. Neither thing is cool. Let the extra seat recline be enough of an award without needing the recognition. Or, you could follow the example of these men and women and just humblebrag about it.

Keith Olbermann (@KeithOlbermann)
Promise not to swamp you but this is breakfast in Delta
1st: Cheerios. MF'ing Cheerios (in coach they get gravel)

The nerve (of you, for posting this)!

🐷 🐷 🐷

Addison Timlin (@Addijay)
The novelty of being flown first class will never wear off, I'm constantly looking around waiting for them to remove me.

The novelty of this tweet wore off very quickly.

BEN BALLER™ (@BENBALLER)
How the fuck do you fart on 1st class? Really c'mon fuck

You wouldn't happen to be implying via a fart, that you are in first class, would you? However, I do find it amusing if Ben Baller (trademark) was sitting in coach, and is just really good at tracing farts. Like Daredevil or something. That was Daredevil's thing, right? He went blind and then could smell farts from afar?

Chris Ziegler (@zpower)
sitting on the tarmac for hours in first class: sucks approximately as much as sitting on the tarmac for hours in coach, turns out.

Agree to disagree!

Al Thornton (@AThornton14)
Its crazy when u the only black person in 1st class all the crazy looks u get.. this guy askd if I was rapper. I said no I'm a swimmer. Lmao

Swimmin' in money that is! From basketball! Which allows you to fly in first class! Which you are humblebragging about!

Jessica Welman (@jesswelman)
First class plane service just blows me away. I don't think

I got as much attention from my own mother when I was a newborn child.

Leave your mother out of this, ma'am!

Wendy Luckenbill (@luckywendy)
American Airlines first class is the equivalent of Virgin's coach. #epicfail AA!

I dunno, Virgin coach is pretty awesome.

Hal Edward Runkel (@HalRunkel)
Even in 1st class, redeyes just suck.

Do not!
(I should mention that after calling him out on this on the feed, Hal wrote an incredibly nice email saying he realizes the error of his ways and that his family was now ragging on him endlessly about it. I felt guilty. So, naturally the next logical thing to do was publish him in the book. Enjoy, Runkels!)

evan turner (@thekidet)
I hate when first class is no diff than coach.
#wasteofmoney

Not a waste at all. You pay more to get to tell people about it.

Kris Allen (@krisallen)
I love how people get freaked out when I don't fly 1st class. On a 45 min flight? Seriously? Not worth it.

Now, this one is interesting because it's about how he is NOT flying first class at the moment, but the rest of the statement implies that for flights over forty-five minutes, he does in fact fly first class. Also, chill out, Kris Allen. No one is freaked out in the slightest. You won a singing contest a long time ago.

Ugh, Being Hot Sure Can Be Annoying!

You know how hot people are the worst? They are. But, what's even worse than that is when they talk about how hot they are. And yet, what's even worse than that—"What?!" you say! "What's worse than *that*," you go on to say! Well, humblebragging about being hot is worse than that. It's worse than anything. Can't they just be content with their finely sculpted bodies and symmetric ear placement! (My ears aren't even. It's a big insecurity of mine. It makes an even sideburn shave a near impossibility.)

Dara Torres (@DaraTorres)
On deck at U of Mizzou getn ready 2 warmup. Some swimmer said "Dara Torres, ur much prettier than I remember!". Is that a compliment? Ha!

Yes. Obviously a compliment!

Megan Ganz (@meganganz)
Someone told me this week that I was so cute, she wanted to "stick me in a Gap ad." Compliment?

Yes. It is inarguably a compliment. What's up with people not knowing what compliments are?

🐷 🐷 🐷

Josh (@jthirsty)
'You look like movie star, hollywood hill.' -asian broken english taxi driver #LAtaxiride

Racist humblebraggery. You are too much, sir!

🐷 🐷 🐷

Colby Prince (@princecolby)
"you're hot!!!" thanks. And thanks for using proper grammar. But I know I look good. Call me cocky, but when you hear it once a day.. Yeah.

On the surface, this may seem like just a regular brag, but the adjective "cocky" is a negative one, thus self-deprecating, thus this guy sucks.

🐷 🐷 🐷

Shaun Phillips (@ShaunPhillips95)
A woman told me i was poetry in motion. I'm not sure how to take that.

With a grain of salt.

Emily Marie (@emwennerberg)
Haha I love when people ask me if I model!!

What's important to know here is that she is not a model, so when people ask her if she is one, it implies that they find her attractive enough to be one. And she fucking loves it.

christina hurricane (@playboybacon)
left the house looking like someone from a theraflu commercial and a dude on broadway declared me "exquisite"....what??

Did you look like someone from a Theraflu commercial before or after they took the Theraflu? This is very pertinent to your question! Please respond!

Jessica Downey (@JessDowney)
I don't like it when guys say things like "since you go on so many dates you should hear that you are hot all the time"

Why? Seriously, why do you dislike that? Also, how many dates are you going on that multiple guys are commenting on the vast number of them? Like four a night? Those are call-girl numbers. Are you a call girl? If so, I can see why it would be annoying for guys to say that to you. I take it back. I take it all back. (My apologies if you aren't a call girl, and in that case, I do not take it back.)

🐷 🐷 🐷

Nicole S. Young (@nicolesy)
Some lady was shocked when I told her my age...she said I look like I'm 23! Lol...I wish. :)

Hells yeah, girl, you put the "young" in Nicole S. Young!

🐷 🐷 🐷

Amanda C. (@antherc)
My office manager told me I should go model for Victoria's Secret. Hahahahahahahahaha!!!! Haven't laughed that hard in a while.

I'm not saying you are, but this tweet makes you seem like a profoundly unpleasant person.

🐷 🐷 🐷

LS (@Torchness)
Just got another random "you look like Reese Weatherspoon." People, just cause we have pointy chins does not make us twins.

Hey, let's not insult Reese just to make your brag seem more self-deprecating.

Jeremy Piven (@jeremypiven)
"U look a million times better in person, I must look like I live in a tree on camera...

No, but your hair is definitely doing weird things on camera.

S. E. Cupp (@secupp)
Just left my Maxim photo shoot. I'm a little nervous about what mom (and Glenn) will say!

Whoa whoa whoa. Who's Glenn?

Holly MacKenzie (@stackmack)
Alison Brie comparisons are always extremely flattering but I don't really see it. I suppose all of us white girls look the same, don't we?

That is not a stereotype about white people.

Single Dad Laughing (@danoah)
I think it's funny how many people told me today that age "definitely made me more attractive." Ummm...thanks. #BackHandedCompliments

#Humblebrags

Jena Friedman (@JenaFriedman)
thank you TSA employee, I do look like a 4 month
pregnant Natalie Portman

Four months isn't even fat yet. You are just saying you look like Natalie Portman.

🐦 🐦 🐦

Donald Glover (@DonaldGlover)
I was shirtless in last nights ep. My name's google alert
this morn was NOTHING but gay porn and teen girl
blogs. I'VE REACHED GLEE STATUS!

Come on, dude.

🐦 🐦 🐦

Shanskiiii ✿ (@gorgeousSHANTI)
I've said dis a million times!!!!! But NO I'm not a model I'm
just really pretty !!!!!!!!!!!!!!

What's important to remember about this tweet (aka the worst thing that has ever happened on earth) is that she also named herself "gorgeous Shanti." Also, regarding the copious usage of exclamation marks: someone may want to go check on her; evidence shows she may have died mid-tweet and her head fell onto the keyboard.

Maggie Q (@MaggieQ)
I AM featured in People's "Most Beautiful" (what can
I say, they all make mistakes) BUT did the shoot w no
makup and I have to say…SCARY!

I'm loving the 3:1 humble-to-brag ratio!

Dominique Piek (@dominiquepiek)
ok…looking for a steamy pic I can post…there are so
many I don't know how to choose! what does this say
about my career? hahaha

That you have a job where you take lewd photos.

Christian Polanco (@chrispolanco)
Was just called gorgeous by a British woman. Boy, the
English sure are stupid.

Weird that he calls his mom "a British woman." SNAP!

Sputnik Sweetheart (@Verlieren)
I'm at the highest risk for being stabbed by a woman when
she asks what my "skin regime" is and I'm like "nothing."

You get any naturally prettier and you're gonna need to go into some sort of government protection program, missy!

QUEENBITCH (@ALLHAILTHEQU33N)
I don't understand why people stare at me. Sorry I wear decent outfits and don't look like all these other hobos.

You answered your own question. Like a beautiful Socrates.

Nat (@TheNatFantastic)
Dear Santa. I know it's early but I really want a male friend I've known for years that doesn't eventually confess they love me. Ta mate x

Hopefully Santa doesn't try to fuck you.

Juliette Lewis (@JulietteLewis)
What not 2do if we meet; Dont say u used to masterbate2me. Never a good opening line to ANYone really. Heard a few times.. Always awkward.

I masturbated to this.

Arianny Celeste (@AriannyCeleste)
Oh an not too mention I have bruises all over..modeling
and acting is not all fun n games folks!! ;)

Did you talk back to the director or something?

Sarah Lacy (@sarahcuda)
my husband just found some site collecting "hot" photos of
me. interestingly enough none include the baby bump…

*Hey, if you're going to say something is interesting, the reader's
expectation is that it's going to be interesting.*

Hipstercrite (@Hipstercrite)
the ONE day i dont wear makeup, everyone comments
on how good my skin looks. makes me feel happy but
wonder if my makeup is usually bad then

Your musings are the worst!

Richard Innes (@bigrichinnes)
A ludicrously hot woman flirted with me on the tube this

morning. I'm now freaking out. I need to be snubbed to get back on an even keel

Define flirting. If you are reading this book, please please please email humblebrag@gmail.com and define flirting.

🐷 🐷 🐷

Owen Pallett (@owenpallett)
A man asked me to have sex with his wife last night. Gross! #StillGotIt

A creepy weirdo thought you were attractive. Still got it indeed.

🐷 🐷 🐷

Stephanie Carpentieri (@jumeauxdemoi)
When guys say to me, "Wow you're actually really smart & funny." What they're really saying is, "You look really stupid & boring."

And what you're really saying is you're really smart and funny.

🐷 🐷 🐷

Tom Lenk (@tomlenk)
Two nights ago I got: "You look like if Patrick Dempsey and Bradley Cooper...." "THANKS!" "Wait - if they had a gay baby." "Um, thanks."

It is bizarre to publicly compare yourself to two of the most univer-
sally attractive people out there. And Tom Lenk knows that deep
down, so he tried to balance it out with some humility—adding the
part about looking like the two of them if they had a gay baby. Mis-
sion unaccomplished! When does being the gay version of something
downgrade its attractiveness? Aren't gay dudes hot? That's, like,
their thing. So by default, the gay baby of Dempsey and Cooper
would be even more good-looking than its heterosexual counterpart.
This humblebrag has failed on multiple levels.

Sidebar: Patrick Dempsey will always be Ronald Miller from
Can't Buy Me Love, *and I don't understand how an entire planet*
of women has collectively forgotten about that and come to label him
Dr. O'Dreamboat or whatever.

🐷 🐷 🐷

Starina Johnson (@StarinaJohnson)
I'm still on the fence as to whether or not it's a compliment
boys I'm old enough to have given birth to think I'm hot.
8-/ #KindaCreepy

Once again, that's a compliment. It can only be construed as a com-
pliment.

🐷 🐷 🐷

Maureen Johnson (@maureenjohnson)
A man at my eye doctor thought I look a lot like Kylie
Minogue. I am glad he is at the eye doctor.

While you're at the doctor, you should get your brag gland checked out. Oh snap!

Dwayne Johnson (@TheRock)
A woman just told me in the gym Im much better lookin in person.. and much meaner lookin too. I should've bit her.

I get the vibe that The Rock is constantly struggling internally with the urge to bite a woman.

Alex Stevens (@astevens389)
I was just told I look like tori amos. Really? I don't quite see it. #random

You are fishing so hard right now, I contemplated mailing you some bait.

KWaites (@WileyWaites)
"You've been lookin good lately, you know, in a really curvy way"…awk.ward.

Yeah, who on earth likes curves on a woman? Oh, everyone? Soooo . . . Not awkward then? K cool.

T (@rollintyler)
Can you guys please stop giving me shit about looking like Jake Gyllenhaal? I didn't ask for any of this.

You brought this on yourself, dude. I didn't even know who you were until you tweeted this and now you're just the guy who looks like Jake Gyllenhaal. You really have only yourself to blame.

Ugh, It's Tough Being a Model

This is a subset of the "I'm hot" genre of humblebrag. And a more annoying one, if you ask me. Models are like hot people, except they get paid for it. (I know. Sucks, right?) They are also quite adept at humblebragging. Observe! (From a distance. And please refrain from feeding them.)

Nate Gill (@NateGill8)
Just bought a house full of groceries and my agent called to tell me I'm leaving town for a week #malemodelproblems

Looks like you'll have to wait a week to vomit up all that food! (Male models are bulimic, too, right?)

🐖 🐖 🐖

carlen altman (@carlenaltman)
See me looking cross-eyed on the Timex website

See me looking roll-eyed at this.

Damaris Lewis (@DamarisLewis)
Leave it up to me to have a drunk man on the train notice that I'm a model, start strutting his stuff…and I join in!!

Ohhhhh, YOU.

But frillz, this is a pet peeve of mine. She is pointing out her own quirkiness here. When girls address their own quirks it means they are aware of it, and that means it's intentional and fabricated, and that makes it annoying and not cute. Damaris started "strutting" on a train, so that she could later tell people about it. A true fun, quirky girl doesn't have to tell people about it. Point being, don't front being quirky, girls!

Trisha Cummings (@Trisha_Cummings)
Walking the runway tonight in a wedding dress, this is a sight that won't be seen again for years to come.

Aw, come on Trisha, there's someone out there for everyone. Even models! I know it's hard to believe, but there are actually men out there who like attractive girls. Hang in there!

Coco Rocha (@cocorocha)
Whats the first thing we models do in Paris? LAUNDRY!!! Just bumped into @Lndsywixson at the laundromat. #PFW #GTLwithouttheT

They're just like us! Oh wait, they're models . . . in . . . Paris.

Jake Pavelka (@jakepavelka1)
Swimsuit photo shoots are like a shot in the arm. Glad
when there over!

*For a guy who apparently doesn't enjoy being in front of the camera,
you sure were voluntarily on five different versions of* The Bachelor!

Eric Lamb (@ICEfluteistnyc)
oh dear.. that's my face on that brochure . . . yikes!

*Brochure models are the worst. Evidently. This is actually the first
time I've ever heard anyone humblebrag about being on a brochure.*

Janice Turner (@VictoriaPeckham)
I am contemplating the extreme horror of having my
photograph taken on Thursday and being "styled"

*If by "contemplating the extreme horror" you mean "telling the
world about it," then yes you are.*

Kristina Shannon (@KristinaShn1)
Good morning tweeties!!! I am soooo sore frm yesterdays
shoot...I swear modeling is just like Advanced Yoga!
hahaha

*In that I hate hearing about either of them? Also, notice how she
added "advanced" to the thing about yoga, casually letting us know
she is in advanced yoga. And also that she is a model. A model who
does advanced yoga and calls people "tweeties"; I would have at
maximum five seconds worth of stuff to talk about with this person.*

Ugh, I'm Too Skinny!

Typically, part of being attractive is being skinny. It's just the standard we have created for ourselves for some reason. But here is the thing about people who humblebrag about being too skinny: I have a gut. So does America. So shut up. I know some people genuinely have a hard time putting on weight, but I have no sympathy for them. All I hear when you say that is that you can eat all the doughnuts you want. And all I want in life is that. I want so many doughnuts so much of the time.

Stephanie Carter (@stephxoxcarter)
My pants keep falling off. I need a smaller size :(

Would a belt work? That's what most people do before jumping right to new pants.

🐖 🐖 🐖

Timothy Prior (@twestp)
getting in shape for no good reason. #habit

I have a habit of chasing cupcakes with cigarettes. I do not understand what you are saying.

Sara E. Makowski Fink (@SaraEMakowski)
I hate buying new clothes when I have so many amazing ones in my closet. The pants situation can't be ignored though. They're too big.

That age old problem: Too many pants, not enough waist fat.

Dana Dearmond (@danadearmond)
I wish these hotel employees would stop staring at me like they've never seen a skinny woman before. Err, or haven't they?

That could be it, or maybe there is a chance they just recognize you from the videos where you have sex with people. (What you need to know here is that Dana Dearmond is a porn star—one of them new-age savvy porn stars, a Sasha Grey type. You know—she's a porn star and stuff, but she also likes Radiohead and Tosh.0.)

All that being said, Dana, I hope this doesn't hurt my chances with you.

Az (@brolf_az)
I find it hard to gain weight. Tips to get fat people! Go!

Foods that have fat in them! Go!

Mike James (@mikejames7)
I'm 199lbs and 4.2% body fat right now. And I'm outta shape.

Mike James is a pro basketball player for the Bulls. The subtext to this tweet is, "Man, can you believe how in shape I am? And I'm out of shape!" He's trying to convey how physically demanding his job is—that he is in pretty amazing physical condition, yet still considers himself out of shape. Arguably one of the all time least relatable gripes on the planet.

Marisa Celine (@MarisaCeline)
"Are you that skinny or do you diet?" haha! What is this diet you speak of? #waituntiliturn25

No one on earth is down with this sentiment.

Sarcastic Meow (@sarcasticmeow)
My favorite pants are too big for me now :(

Just get smaller pants and enjoy not having a fat ass anymore, like a normal person. Or once again: A BELT! Why can't newly skinny people wrap their heads around the belt?

Brooke Burke (@brookeburke)
Shipping for bikinis with my daughter. Omg! Were the same size. I'm in biiig trouble!

Okay, assuming Brooke Burke meant "shopping" instead of "shipping," why is she in big trouble??? Is it, like, one of those "Uh-oh! My daughter is the same size as me and I'm a model. Here come the boys! Watch out!" type things? If so, Brooke Burke is essentially calling herself hot and petite.

Or she's calling her daughter freakishly huge, which isn't a humblebrag, but also isn't nice and she should be admonished for it.

Ugh, People Keep Hitting on Me!

And so if we follow this path a little farther—being attractive naturally leads to being hit on. Who doesn't like being hit on? Feels nice to be wanted, right? Wrong, apparently. People are frequently tweeting about how annoying it is that they were just hit on. But they must take SOME satisfaction from it, right? I mean, otherwise, they wouldn't tweet about it to the whole world, right? Sometimes in this category, the offender openly enjoys being hit on and just can't understand why it happened when they looked their "worst." So, basically they were given a compliment by the person coming on to them and are then tweeting about it with the hope of inevitably receiving more compliments (i.e., I'm sure you looked beautiful, grrrrl). Lame.

> **Donovan** (@LadyDonovan)
> OBSERVATION: I receive more attention from men when I'm wearing a hat. CONCLUSION: I look tons better with half of my face covered.

The top of your head is not half of your face. Are you wearing a half-ski mask? Is that a thing?

Nadia Quinn (@nadiaquinn)
Lots of young boys & also old men get crushes on me.
And tell me (or their moms do). What does this say,
exactly?

*That you got it goin' on, grrrl! Right? I mean, that's what you
meant, right?*

kdn (@kdn13)
Given I look like a 13 year old boy in my work out clothes,
I'm certain the men who pick up on me at the gym are all
pedophiles.

*Pedophiles? I've got good mind to call the police. On YOU—for
lookin' so hot always!*

Ms. Miranda (@JennyMariePR)
Why do men hit on me more when I'm in sweat pants? It
makes no sense.

*Truly one of the world's greatest unsolved mysteries. In fact, I hand-
wrote a letter to Robert Stack to see if he can figure it out. If he
doesn't respond, I'll ask Dennis Farina. (He hosted* Unsolved
Mysteries *after Robert Stack. Weird, right?)*

Chelsy McInnis (@chelsysayshi)
Am I giving out some kind of "ask me on a date vibe?" I
was under the impression that I was giving a "fuck off I'm
eating" vibe. Go away.

I can tell you what vibe you're giving off...

Yemyoom (@yemmeyummy)
I'm insulted whenever random guys ask for my number. It
makes me feel cheap. Like who do you think I am?

Okay wait, I feel very confused at why this makes you feel cheap.
Presumably you want guys to take you out on real dates, proper-
style, whilst courting you. But wouldn't they have to call you in order
to plan said date? How is merely asking for your number insulting?
Unless these guys are saying to you, "Can I have your number so I
can call you for random sex at 2:30 a.m. after I hit up Jack in the
Box with my boyz?" But I don't think they're saying that.

Tricia Adams (@Trish1981)
No makeup on, hair's not done, toothpaste stains
down the front of my shirt, pretty sure I'm not wearing
deodorant. Still get hit on. *sigh*

It's probably because they didn't realize those stains were toothpaste.

Colin Cabalka (@ccabalka)
Worst thing about shooting weddings: Drunk girls that
try to hit on me. #classy

Ugh, the worst. (I'm talking about photographers.)

Crissy Henderson (@crissyhenderson)
super random- but i never wear my hair curly and i did
today-- I've had more looks and whistles than i know how
to handle…#confused

That is SUPES RANDO! Thanks for sharing!

Amy Lorraine (@AmesLorraine)
I'm wearing a ponytail,rolled out of bed from a nap, at the
bar w/ my guy and guys r still hitting on me. Like really??

Seriously, what are dudes' problems??

Jamie O'Brien ♬ (@LoveJamieO)
Seriously?! My hair is curly as fuck, I'm wearing a giant
sweatshirt, pants, uggs, sunglasses & no makeup & still
get honked ml hollered at

Really? Even while your hair is curly as fuck??? Guys hate hair that is curly as fuck!! That is a known fact!!! May as well smear shit on your face!

🐷 🐷 🐷

McKenzie Coburn (@McKenzieCoburn)
How many times can u reject a guy before he gets the hint? Said no 3x and even pulled the lesbian card Which I NEVER have done #getthehint

Have you tried not being so irresistibly beautiful?

🐷 🐷 🐷

Mandi Crotty (@mandicrotty)
Alright getting hit on by the comcast guy is a little unsettling at 9am. Especially since I'm in sweats, ponytail and no makeup

Haven't you seen porn? You were supposed to sleep with that fellow! Quit fucking up the fantasy!

🐷 🐷 🐷

Sofia Noethe (@fiakealii)
Why must men leer out the windows of their car at me when I walk places?? It's effing terrifying. #respectplease

Aretha Franklin over here!

Marissa Maharaj (@marissamaharaj)
Got asked out during my eighth hour of shooting. A little
flattered, mostly confused. #8thHourAintPretty

*You mean you got hit on after eight hours of hair and makeup people
constantly tending to you? This could be the one.*

🐷 🐷 🐷

Stacey A. (@CurvesAndNerves)
I declare today to be called "City Workers Are Actively
Hitting On Stacey Even Though She Just Woke Up And
Looks It" Day.

*Sorry, it's already National Tree Planting Day (in Australian schools—
I looked it up).*

🐷 🐷 🐷

Kamilah Anwar (@KamilahAnwar)
This group of bum looking guys just tried hitting on me in
front of all of my co-workers. Hilarious & embarrassing at
the same time

*Well, it's happened: the most hateable thought that has ever been
conveyed by man. From her profile picture Kamilah looks to be some
sort of model-type person I guess, or at the very least, she appears to
be standing how a model stands. "This group of bum-looking guys"
makes this the worst/funniest right off the bat. And then she goes on
to be embarrassed at the mere idea of someone who looks like a homeless person giving her attention. It's like, "Yeah, right, homeless guy!*

*I'm fucking Kamilah Anwar and you don't have a fucking home!
Keep it movin', pal!"*

Boo, Kamilah Anwar. Boo to you.

Emma Lenchner (@em_lench)
The next person to whistle at me, cat call me or even
look me up and down with is gonna have another thing
coming to them, probably my fist

I gotta say, you threatening me is kinda hot. 'Sup?

Ugh, I Hate Having All This Money!

If there's anything more annoying than people bragging about their attractiveness, it's bragging about how rich they are. Or maybe they're equally annoying. In any case, you'd think at this point in society, every single person would know it is tacky to discuss matters of finance. But nope. People do it a lot. And why? Maybe they're bored. If that is the case, here are a plethora of activities you can do instead of tweeting to the world that you are rich: buy a bunch of cars, buy a bunch of boats, buy a house for each season, invent a new season and buy a house for it, buy happiness, etc. Point being, there have to be ways outside of humblebragging on Twitter to enjoy your riches.

Daniel Negreanu (@RealKidPoker)
Is it weird that I actually enjoy cleaning someone else's apt? I never get to at home thanks to @dnassistant so it's kinda fun!

You made your assistant's Twitter name be "dnassistant"? Isn't that kind of a complete dick move? Also, on behalf of maids everywhere: Ew.

Sam Simon (@simonsam)
Rats ate the wiring of my Tesla. It's gonna cost $50,000 to fix. I'm sure you all know the feeling.

You cocreated the Simpsons, so I know you'll understand this, but that was, like, something Mr. Burns would say. Not cool, man.

Michael Muhney (@michaelmuhney)
I also remember as a kid thinking, "When I grow up & have lots of $$ I'm buying MC Hammer pants in every color!" I was also wrong about that

About what? Having lots of $$? I can't really blame the guy, though. After all, his last name is money.

Tobias Lütke (@tobi)
I just started writing a tool that I know I could turn into another million dollar company if I had the time.

In related news, you just started being a tool that has enough time to tweet shit like this.

Tony Hawk (@tonyhawk)
In my quest for culinary adventures, I had cave swift bird nest soup last night. $150 for mediocre slop, lame.

Tony, remember being fourteen and getting kicked out of parking lots for grinding on benches and stuff? You have gotten so far away from that.

🐷 🐷 🐷

Evan Lysacek (@EvanLysacek)
Why do I always get gassy limo drivers?

Why do you always get limos?

🐷 🐷 🐷

Aubrey O'Day (@AubreyODay)
Is it wrong that im a lil white girl in a bmw driving through bel air bumpin Thugish Rugish Bone…& singin it as hard as the chick in it?

I don't know. Never really thought about the issue 'til you brought it up. But, offhand, I'd say, yes, everything you are doing is wrong.

🐷 🐷 🐷

Alex Baze (@bazecraze)
Mom's very first words today "Well, you don't look rich. Is that the idea?" #mauiwithmom

So the unmentioned beginning of this conversation had to have been you saying, "I'm rich."

Oney Guillen (@Oneyguillen)
In the limo riding to airport. Sucks being alone though

Well, luckily it's only for the duration of a limo ride. If you can't be alone for that short stretch of time, there are more serious issues at play here. Also, you're not alone, because who is driving the limo? Or do you not consider limo drivers to be people? Waiiiiiit a minute, I get what's happening here: You ARE the limo driver on the way to pick someone up at the airport, and you refer to "the limo" like an old ball and chain, the way people say "the Chevy" or something. If that is the case, my insincerest apologies.

BEST COAST (@bestycoastyy)
Holy shit my hotel room in Brisbane is bigger than my entire house!

More like Best BOAST! Sounds like your career is on fire and you'll get that big house in no time. (Frillz, I hope I'm right. Their music is pretty good and I want nothing but good things for them).

Garrett Wolfe (@GWolfe25)
Ordered Room service n it was 100 pounds #fml

"#fml" is Internet speak for "fuck my life." By the time this book comes out, people won't be saying it anymore, probably. This tweet is a time capsule of sorts.

justonius hookius (@justinhook)
The fact a single one of my paychecks exceeds the daily limit for smartphone deposits isn't so much flattering as it is TYPICAL BANK SHIT.

Prolly could have kept all of these thoughts in the ol' noggin, eh?

Tech N9ne (@TechN9ne)
Hey @kenyewest & @jayz I'm sure you niggas know, so how do I clean black diamonds? Is it like u clean regular ones?

Humblebrag or otherwise, this is one of the best things that has ever been said. (Also, I like that he calls him "Kenye." Guess it's a rapper thing.)

Kara Alesandra (@KaraAlesandra)
Well, my Mercedes got me a speeding ticket. Damn Lady Cops! LOL

You seem stoked about it.

Jaleel White (@jaleelwhite)
NEW ETIQUETTE ALERT: If u don't greet ur own limo at

precisely the time, ur driver will leave U like a jet @ the
arport #TAXI

Urk-dawg relating to the people!

Darren Carter (@darrencarter)
I hate when the limo is late. They say to call after we get
our bags. Next time I'm calling when I board the plane

LOLOLOLOLvomit.

Jared Followill (@youngfollowill)
Mother of God. Tornado coming. Hide in my wine cellar
or my theatre? Or my gym. (in the face of death, I still find
ways to brag)

*That you do, King of Leon, that you do. My two cents: You may
want to hide in the band practice room. That last album was a little eh.*

George Cunningham (@georgeherbertc)
seals woke me up. the bittersweet of #yachtliving

*If you ever say or type the phrase "yacht living," you should reevalu-
ate what is important to you in your life.*

Peter Shankman (@petershankman)
Dear NYC: "Mansion Tax??" It's a F*cking TWO
BEDROOM APARTMENT!!!!" #feelingBloomberged

*You know two bedrooms in New York is, like, pretty big, right? Most
people have to live in a closet or an ATM vestibule.*

Shaycarl (@shaycarl)
It doesn't matter how much granite, marble tile, jacuzzi
tub or square footage a hotel room has…if the internet is
slow then it SUCKS!

I dunno, sounds pretty nice.

Rashard Mendenhall (@R_Mendenhall)
I often daydream about burning all the money I've made.
That way the selfish people around me will be forced to
talk about something else…

You're the one tweeting about it, bruh.

Lily Morrow (@LilyMorrow21)
Great, bentley has flat tire, now taking a cab : (second
problem with that car this week!!

You should maybe splurge for Triple A. Just saying. If you got the Bentley, may as well spend the extra, like fifty bucks?

Steven Haddadian (@StevenHaddadian)
There's this dance move I learned today called the agent. Its when your client books a $9 million project & then you do this retarded dance

You're fired.

[Christofer] Hoff (@Beaker)
Meh. Tesla in-stock inventory not meeting what I want and I don't want to custom build/order a long lead car being discontinued. Blah.

I love the "Meh" "Blah" bookends on this with the killer Tesla brag in the middle. Well done, sir.

Seeby Woodhouse (@seeby)
Just bought a couple of VIP tickets to the Semi-finals and final games of the #RWC2011 - $25,000 later…ouch…

That actually is a shit ton of money to spend on a sporting event. I'd probably tell people about it, too. Just kidding—gross!

Robert Janofsky (@RobJanof)
Maids leave my house so I can go workout!!!
#Takingforever

"Maids" plural? Just workout by lifting your wallet!

Bam Margera (@BAM__MARGERA)
Broken down lambo, raaaaaad!

The Jackass guys have made more money than pretty much anyone on earth and they did so by allowing snakes to bite their penises and obaco mon to sweat into their mouths. And I honestly think they deserve every cent. No single piece of art makes me happier than Jackass. So, Bam, buy a thousand lambos, and humblebrag about each one of them. I don't give a shit. Just keep making movies.

Ugh, It's Hard Being So Charitable!

I remember one time several years ago, my roommate asked me to drive him to the airport at like 5 a.m. Normally I'd be like "yeah!" but it was 5 a.m., so I was like, "Can I just give you cab fare instead? I'd rather sleep in and pay a fee." He then guilted me by saying he'd do the same for me. I ended up driving him, but it didn't even feel like I was helping a friend out, since I had just bitched about it. I should have shut up and done it all along.

My point is, if you are going to give to charity, don't fucking talk about it. It ruins the whole good deed.

Van Durham (@vandurham)
I was told I saved someone's life today. But really, I was just doing my job.

Fine, I'll give you the response you want: No, you are a hero. There. Happy?

🐷 🐷 🐷

Steven Jackson (@sj39)
Sending my nephews and nieces to college is $$$$…but it's worth it. I love them.

If this was on Yelp, that would be the maximum number of dollar signs! You are a saint!

Steve Szlaga (@Szzzzlaga)
I run marathons for cancer. I mentor elementary school students. I mention Ke$ha MAYBE once a week. Guess which thing I'm best known for.

Being a blowhard?

Ric Bucher (@RicBucher)
aka, Juror No.3 for next two weeks. Knew what to say to get boot, saw/heard others say it. Just couldn't. #howhavingaconsciencecansuck.

Too bad your incredible conscience couldn't kick in when you were thinking about tweeting this.

phil_hellmuth (@phil_hellmuth)
Police stopped me 4 speeding; 1st thought, "I raised $1 million 4 police doing charity events!" 2thought "Please Phil, no 1 is abve the law"

Was your third thought throwing yourself off a bridge?

Cameron Sinclair (@casinclair)
Dammit we are completing projects quicker than I can
up them on the @archforhumanity website. 2 schools and
250 homes...egads.

This one actually made me stop for a second and feel guilty about calling them out for doing genuinely good deeds. That is a lot of schools and homes. But still, starting with "dammit" makes it a bona fide humblebrag and I have a snarky book to write! So, deal with it, Cameron Sinclair!

Matt Nordgren (@MattNordgren)
Setting up your own charity and event is no joke. Would
have thought it to be easier...this serious

But think about the reward. Just think about the day when you can look back and tell people about how you set up a charity event.

Cheryl Yeoh (@cherylyeoh)
I just did something very selfless. But more importantly, it
was genuine & I know it means a lot to the person in the
long run #soworthit

You know that tweeting this not only erases the good deed you did, but any other good thing you've ever done in your entire life? Sorry. Sucks.

Clarke Thomas (@needcaffeine)
WTF!? now charities are calling me at home to thank me
for my donation. just send me a letter, thanks

*If they wanted to send you a letter, what address would they need to
send that to? I *promise* I won't egg your house.*

Braylon Edwards (@OfficialBraylon)
It's no fun being successful all by yourself! I try to place
everyone around me in a better situation if I can

*This is very kind and noble of you—whoops, sorry, typo: I meant
annoying and embarrassing of you.*

Troy Sutton (@StrengthCoachT)
gave away way too much money to homeless people last
night. I need to start factoring them into my monthly budget.

*You should also start factoring modesty serum into your budget. I'm
well aware that nothing called "modesty serum" exists. But if science
ever makes it, you should def factor it into your budget.*

Bryce Avary (@TheRocketSummer)
Honestly choked up from lyrics that just came to me. It's

an amazing moment when you know that a song is going to help someone.

Honestly choked up (with vomit) from reading this.

Dina Manzo (@dinamanzo)
I obsess over the welfare of old people & animals on hot days like today. OBSESS #thereissomethingwrongwithme

Oh you hush, Real Housewife of New Jersey. The only thing wrong with you is that you have the heart of an angel, and then also all the other unlikable shit about you.

Ugh, Being an Author Is Hard!

As opposed to the wealthy humblebraggers of that last couple of sections, here we have a group not typically known for being so flush with cash: the lonesome writer. You'd think that years of rejection and nobody caring about their work would make them fairly humble, but no. I don't know what it is about authors, but they are some of the worst offenders in the game. My theory is that it's because no one really recognizes authors or knows what they look like. They aren't getting shouted at on any street corners for any autographs, so their horn toots must solely come from themselves. Luckily I do other things besides this book, or I'd probably turn into a real monster. (Humblebrag! Just keeping you on your toes.)

Also, did you know that every person ever is an author?

Sarah Palin (@SarahPalinUSA)
Inexplicable: I recently won in court to stop my book "America by Heart" from being leaked, but US Govt can't stop Wikileaks' treasonous act?

Have you ever said anything that anyone liked? Serious question.

Michael Waltrip (@mw55)
just tried to pre-order my book. couldnt figure it out. did
anyone try?

No.

Dave Itzkoff (@ditzkoff)
RTing as a fan. Not b/c they like my book too RT
@pattonoswalt 1 month til my book is released.
PENTHOUSE liked it

Piggybacking on someone else's humblebrag. I like it!

Merlin Mann (@hotdogsladies)
Sitting alone at a table in Starbucks, writing a book on
a MacBook Air. Because I'm a triple venti douchenozzle
with room for cream.

*If you truly thought you were a "douchenozzle," you wouldn't have
typed this to the world. You think you're kiiiinda cool.*

Russell Simmons (@UncleRUSH)
I dont rlly celebrate "achievement" nor suffer so much ovr
"failure" but #SuperRich is now officially my 2nd nytimes
best seller

So, you're . . . celebrating . . . achievement?

Chris Hardwick (@nerdist)
Well, after a 3 hour delay, an aborted approach and a landing that felt like Star Tours, HELLLLO NY! (no shows, just book meetings)

Meetings plural, y'allllll . . .

Gary Vaynerchuk (@garyvee)
I am starting to feel like the @nyjets #2- two years in a row :(#NYTimes #2 #bestsellers list

With a frowny face emoticon to boot! Gross!

Bill Simmons (@sportsguy33)
I'd like to thank Random House for making sure my book is never available in any airport or train station bookstore. Always feels good.

Bill Simmons lets me write on his website and even provided a blurb for this book, so I won't rag on him too hard (I just humblebragged while critiquing someone's humblebrag—this is like an M. C. Escher painting!), but this is indeed a humblebrag.

Hayley Williams (@yelyahwilliams)
When you walk into a bookstore and your face is
everywhere and you look a lot better in the pic than you
do right now…#hahaha #crazylife

*When you say that your "face is everywhere," I promise no one
wants to hear the rest of what you have to say.*

Rebecca Boston (@bostonita)
Realizing I'm every copywriter's worst nightmare. Im
never pleased! In my head, things sound better cuz I pull
words from 3+ languages!

*I think the humility must have gotten lost somewhere in translation
or something. Also, what's all this plus sign business? Don't leave
us hanging! How many languages are you pulling from precisely!?*

Jillian Barberie (@askjillian)
Meeting with book agent cancelled today I don't know
what to do with myself!!!!

*I don't know what you should do with yourself, either, but tweeting
this was probably a misstep.*

Michio Kaku (@michiokaku)
On my book tour, I just scored a new record. I signed

210 books in one night (at the univ. in Minneapolis). But it took over an hour!

Pretty boring record!

🐦 🐦 🐦

Tucker Max (@TuckerMax)
Girl:"My fav band is the backstreet boys, my fav tv show is gossip girl and my fav book is yours!" Me:"I've failed as a human."

Agree to agree!

🐦 🐦 🐦

Ayelet Waldman (@ayeletw)
What I'm dealing with: Book tour, deadline 4 novel, 4 musical, 4 screenplay, 4 collection of narratives, new house. And oh yeah 4 kids.

4 humblebrags! (I don't consider kids or musicals as things to brag about.)

🐦 🐦 🐦

Keli Goff (@keligoff)
Despite being pretty used 2 tv I still get all kinds of NERVOUS at book readings. Is that weird?

That you're on TV? Yeah.

Richard Wiseman (@RichardWiseman)
Just been recognised whilst buying my own book. Well
that wasn't embarrassing then.

This was!

Megatron McLush (@MsGinnis)
..did I just get offered a book deal? I'm too tired to
comprehend

Get some sleep and let us know. Pins and needles over here.

Robert J Wiersema (@robertjwiersema)
Fuck. I wrote a memoir. #whatwasIthinking
#interviewpanic

*This interview will make for good fodder for memoir #2, ami-
right????*

David Yelland (@davidyelland)
Saw someone leaf through my novel in
Waterstones earlier and *put it back on the shelf*
#imstillfollowingthemcallthepolice

You hang out by your own book in bookstores?

Chris Brogan (@chrisbrogan)
On the phone with my editor, book publicist, and
marketing person. Man, books take work. Mainstream
ones.

TMI.

🐛 🐛 🐛

Nicholas Kristof (@NickKristof)
Hmm. @Amazon won't let me order more than 3 copies
of "Half the Sky." Is that a new limit on discounted best-
sellers? Anybody know?

*I'm more than confident that Amazon could field that question
for you.*

Totes McGotes

I don't know who the Twitter user @TotesMcGotes is, but he has changed my life for the better. In the early stages of the Humblebrag experiment, someone I don't know sent me a tweet by this man. The tweet was as follows:

Actually have to dolly my tv through the house. Like a 4mile walk from garage to family/pool room.

It was a perfect humblebrag. The brag was about his new TV and his massive mansion (the complaint being that his house is TOO big to carry a TV through). After poking around on this guy's Twitter page, I still knew nothing about him, except that he communicated almost exclusively through humblebragging. I didn't know what he did for a job and I still don't. I know it must be lucrative, because most of his tweets are about expensive material possessions.

Totes is too prolific a humblebragger to not have a chapter of his own. I now present you . . . Totes McGotes.

I can bench like crazy, jog the highest stairs, lift heaviest of objects but tweak my neck or pull a muscle while reaching for a snack?!?

I wonder what the highest stairs he's ever jogged are. There aren't that many around to begin with. Like football stadiums I guess? Or like ancient Mayan temples?

Jesus. I go out for food gas and end up buying all new snowboarding gear and a new LCD TV and surround sound receiver. #earlyblackfriday

What do regular people impulse-buy? Batteries? Us Weeklys? Fuck that. Totes McGotes impulse buys TVs and snowboarding gear!

Who wants a side gig of helping me clean this house? DM me if interested. My usual lady says it's too big (thats what she said). #job $$$

Just putting it out there for all the maids on Twitter who follow an anonymous man named Totes McGotes.

Told the cpl renting my house in the midwest, who both lost their jobs last month, not to worry about Nov/Dec rent. They have a little boy.

The grossest way possible to tell us that he owns property in the Midwest.

Maybe I'm too nice, but stories like that around the holidays get to me. Hopefully they'll give their little boy a good xmas. #karma

This is a continuation of the previous tweet about the Midwest family. It is very confusing to me. He is getting choked up by his own story about himself? What??

Screw the power nap…gonna take one of the toys on a sunset cruise #decisions #worksmarterplayharder

Anyone over the age of eight, shouldn't call anything a "toy."

Tipped the 4 people working last night $100 each. Awesome food they stayed open just for us and it's the holiday. I feel good.

You feel good about telling people this.

Omg so tired. Long day ahead but I know as soon as I'm on the boat my happiness level will increase 90%...hope to spot some killer whales!

Anyone who calls "a" boat "the" boat, needs to not do that.

Lived in this house 9mos and I've yet to use all 0 of the bathrooms. This will have to change in 2011. It's good to have goals. #dreambigger

Good luck in your future wealthy shits!

I just realized I've only showered in ONE of my FIVE showers since I've moved in here. This must change #totesproblems

Noticing a theme here.

Sent my personal assistant to the liquor store with $300 cash...I'm not sure I'd ever come back if I were her. :)

You'd retire with three hundred dollars? You are terrible with money. How'd you get so rich?

Some snow bunny took my number this evening and she already texted me. Stage 5 clinger...

"Snow bunny"? Uch.

Making house payments and stuff...flippin ouch. Some days I miss the condo....but the house is 102% more fun.

Occupy Totes Street.

Still remember buying a domain for $100 back in the late 90s and selling it for $60k just months later. Capital gains suck. #dotcom

I don't know what any of that means starting with "capital gains," but I definitely feel like it's a humblebrag.

I should sleep...my personal assistant is going to be here bright and early tomorrow #whiteguyproblems

Attention all nonwhite people, please don't think Totes speaks for all of us, thank you.

Preparing my accountant for my office changing from a few hundred sq ft to several thousand. And boat expenses as third home. #plsdontaudit

Please audit him.

The DMs thanking me for inspiration and motivation are too much some days. You guys rock! I promised myself I wouldn't cry...

Who did you inspire to do what exactly, Totes? Who even knows your actual name?

Jesus christ. My gas bill for the last month...over $,2000. Sucks having a heated pool/spa and not the time of year for solar.

This is like a parody of a Totes McGotes's humblebrag.

Not going to be able to sleep. Hope to close this piece of business by monday making Jan & Feb record revenue months for my companies!

What companies? Please God what companies!

Being self-made is scary as hell sometimes. But the rewards are incredible! Take a risk. Find true happiness.

You heard it here: You don't know what fear is until you've been self-made!

Preparing for my meeting with Oprah. This was nowhere on my goals list for 2011. Life wins! #hopeigetafreegift

Oprah got to meet Totes?!??

Propane is up to almost $4/gal and my tank holds 1000 gallons to heat pool/spa...I go through a tank every 2 weeks. ouch. #totesproblems

This is like a math problem on the Shithead SATs.

Yes!! Comped penthouse suite in Vegas on a Holiday Weekend. I would feel good about that but just means I gamble too damn much :(

Ah come on, you feel great. You're Totes and Totes feels great.

Not gonna lie there's powdered sugar sprinkled throughout the penthouse. The maids will get a good chuckle

I hope the maids get a better chuckle than we got. I feel a little gypped chuckle-wise, as long as we're being honest.

Not sure what my growing up ghetto ass did to deserve
a waterfront place in SoCal with bikinis around all day,
but thank you baby Jesus.

Which ghetto? Laguna? Ojai?

There you have it. Totes in a nutshell.

I once reached out to Totes to see if he would be willing
to let me stay at his mansion for a weekend in San Diego. He
was totally game, but our schedules never lined up. Mostly
because he is pretty much always in Las Vegas. I have never
seen anyone be in Las Vegas more than this man.

To some degree, I'm relieved I never met him. I don't
really want to know his real name or his occupation. I don't
want to know the person behind the Totes. To me, he's just
Totes McGotes and that's how I like it.

Totes has stopped humblebragging for the most part. He
became too aware of the concept, I think. At one point, I
didn't retweet him for a whole month and he tweeted something like "I forgot to feed the machine this month" (referring to humblebrag). Then, he tried to bait me with a couple
of softballs, like this one:

One of my good friends is on Undercover Boss tonight.
Weird. They are kind of portraying him as a dick so far tho.

It was just too pitch-perfect to be authentic. I want genuine Totes. So, my new plan is to just leave him alone and
pretend I forgot about him. Eventually, he'll fall back into

his old habits. He has to. And if not, at least I can cherish the Totes memories I do have.

Here's to you, Totes.

★★★★★It should be noted that since I was devoting an entire chapter of the book to Totes, I figured I should reach out to Totes and ask if he was cool with that. He said he was cool, but in exchange he wanted to be the only person that the @humblebrag account follows on Twitter. I typically don't negotiate with terrorists, but it was a small price to pay for the riches he's bestowed upon all of us.

Once again: To TOTES!★★★★★

"Weird"/"Awkward"/"Surreal"

A very popular form of humblebraggery is saying a brag and then tacking on the word "weird," "awkward," or "surreal." But they ain't fooling no one.

Go ahead and try it with any brag. It's fun...

I just won a million dollars. Weird.
I just won an Oscar. Awkward.
I just had sex with Kate Middleton and William was totally cool with it. Surreal.

This is definitely the laziest form of humblebragging, but it's always hilarious. Especially since most of the time, it isn't weird at all.

James Van Der Beek (@vanderjames)
It's weird passing on job offers when you have a kid...
worse though, would be taking time away from her to
work on the wrong job, I think.

Okay, okay, we get it, Beek. You're still in high demand. Jeez Louise.

Rev Run (@RevRunWisdom)
Feels weird layin in ur bed watchin ur self layin in bed…
Watchin #runshouse

Some classic wisdom from the Rev! Hey, man, "If it feels weird, don't do it," I always say.

🐑 🐑 🐑

Nikki Sixx (@NikkiSixx)
At EMI party at Milk. Paps just said "I like your hair". I told them i have had the same cut for over 20 years. Awkward.

Yooo, love Mötley Crüe. Big fan. But nothing about that exchange is awkward.

🐑 🐑 🐑

Peter Facinelli (@peterfacinelli)
Was introduced to a man named Michael at a meeting. I said "you look familiar, have we met"? Turns out it was Michael Bay. oops. #awkward

Relatable.

🐑 🐑 🐑

Eddie Trunk (@EddieTrunk)
Weird to hear myself right now on Sirius XM while driving down Sunset Blvd.

What is it about Sunset Boulevard that makes this scenario particularly weird for you, friend?

RuPaul (@RuPaul)
Just passed my billboard on Sunset Blvd - After all these
years, I still ask myself "is that me?" #Surreal

After all the work you've had done on yourself, I can understand the confusion.

Terence Wiggins (@TheBlackNerd)
Sometimes I think it's really weird that I have a comic.
And that people read it. And like it.

What about the other times?

Arian Foster (@ArianFoster)
It's still surreal to me that people take their hard earned
money to purchase my jersey. Everyone I see a 23
walking around I smile.

Hey, don't just assume that their money is hard-earned. I'm sure there are plenty of people spending their easily earned money on an Arian Foster jersey. And also probably a fair number of people spending no money on an Arian Foster jersey.

jeph jacques (@jephjacques)
They're doing a "celebrity bartender" thing at the local pub. Very weird to realize that I'm more "famous" than any of the "celebrities."

Even weirder to talk about it. Also, I gotta say I agree with him. Who is this person?

Paul Armstrong (@wiseacre)
I cannot tell you how weird it is to see yourself big on screen, it's weird.

We get it—it's weird.

Peter Atencio (@Atencio)
Also it's weird to be sitting on 10+ amazing sketches that I can't share with the internet. TV is like a really bad case of blue balls.

Hopefully by the time this book came out you got to ejaculate those sweet sweet sketches onto America's face.

🐦 🐦 🐦

lauren flax (@laurenflax)
lol just heard my song for the first time in the new Kmart commercial #lifeisweird

How so specifically?

🐦 🐦 🐦

Jamal Crawford (@JCrossover)
Just met President Obama, and he know who I was..
WOW#surreal!

You would think at a certain point, NBA players would start getting used to being recognized, seeing as how every single person on the planet (including small villages in Eastern Europe with no televisions) and also dogs and birds love the NBA. But nope, they are always surprised. Even though athletes are basically celebrities for celebrities. Jack Nicholson watches Kobe play every night.

🐦 🐦 🐦

Dorothy Robinson (@dorothyatmetro)
This week: Interviewing Seinfeld then going to a tequila

and tacos party with Lil Jon. It is a weird world we live in, folks.

I bet neither of those men know you by name.

🐷 🐷 🐷

Sam Halliday (@samhallidayTDCC)
Our song has just come on the radio in our taxi. Awkward!

Why is that awkward? I assure you the cabdriver doesn't know you're the band that is on the radio.

🐷 🐷 🐷

hollyburns @hollyburns
I'm at Paula Deen's house. HOUSE. My life is so weird!

Seems normal—wait, her house??? HOUSE?!?? Never mind! AHHHHHH!!!!!!!

🐷 🐷 🐷

Reggie Bush (@reggie_bush)
In the Adidas Store is it weird if I buy my own cleats???

Do you need cleats? Then, no.

Derek matarangas (@dmimage)
I find it weird that I'm signing my work now.

That's on you, bro!

Pauly Poltergeist (@Drapht)
That awkward moment when you're sitting in KFC drive through ordering and your song comes on.

You could've ended that after "KFC drive through." The rest of it actually wasn't that awkward.

James Nelan (@cubbyhappenings)
There is something decidedly strange about listening to your own song on the radio while you are at your day job.

Whoa whoa whoa. Who decided this?

Travis Beacham (@travisbeacham)
It's still surreal seeing "Pacific Rim" in headlines—a title that just kinda fell into my head when I was walking on the beach one day.

Wait, so this back-pat is for coming up with a title that was just the place you were standing? I call bullshit.

Adam Liaw (@adamliaw)
Guy sitting next to me is reading a magazine article with a big picture of me in it. Awkward.

Who cares.

a michelle (@ahaarttt)
Some woman just screamed at me from across the street "you have pretty hair!!" long range compliments are awkward and kind of scary.

So awkward and scary you had to rush to a computer and proudly tweet it.

Marjorie Totten (@marjorietotten)
That awkward moment when you look like Diaz in Bad Teacher washing your car. #uncomfortablestares

Comparing yourself to Cameron Diaz is never becoming on anybody.

Matt Jones (@mattjonesisdead)
I was just on TMZ. Weird…

I feel like you were just baiting me with this one. Ah well, mission accomplished.

🐑 🐑 🐑

Jesse Hall (@Jhall2121)
It's weird I feel too young to be flying on the corporate jet.
Oh well ill get on anyway.

So lame. What you just did is SO lame.

🐑 🐑 🐑

Edo (@edojao)
Guy at Klay just came up to me and said "You don't look like the pictures, you are even better." Weirded out.

What's Kla—ah, fuggit. Nevermind. Don't care. Congratulations. Great job.

Humblebrags from Throughout History

As previously stated, humblebrags do not exist solely on Twitter, nor do they exist solely in our time period. I wanted to include a wide variety of humblebrags from many different time periods as a testament to how deeply ingrained within us humblebrags have always been. Eve probably humblebragged to Adam about how she hates her apple diet or whatever (I don't really know the Bible that well).

Genghis Khan

"With Heaven's aid I have conquered for you a huge empire. But my life was too short to achieve the conquest of the world. That task is left for you."

Genghis said this to his son upon his deathbed. I bet his son was all, "Ughhh, here we go again with the 'conquered a huge empire and now I have to take over the entire world' thing for the umpteenth time. I get it, Dad. Jeez."

Napoleon Bonaparte

"What I have done up to this is nothing. I am only at the beginning of the course I must run."

That's a quote from his memoirs. And the "nothing" that he is referring to is merely becoming the emperor of France. Some people don't even make it up to assistant manager at FedEx Kinko's in their lifetime.

🐷 🐷 🐷

Albert Einstein

Albert Einstein is the guy they based the movie *I.Q.* on.

"The more success the quantum theory has, the sillier it looks."

Arguably the nerdiest Humblebrag of all time. We GET it— your quantum theory that light exists as photons is successful! Gawd!

"With fame I become more and more stupid, which, of course, is a very common phenomenon."

Question: Who said this: Paris Hilton or Albert Einstein? Answer: It was Einstein! I KNOW, right?

"Do not worry about your difficulties in mathematics; I can assure you that mine are still greater."

Okay, Einstein! (I've always wanted to say that commonly used expression to Einstein himself. Mission accomplished.)

Al Capone

Al Capone really revolutionized the Mafia-humblebrag.

"The news gang are forever riding me. Seems as if I'm responsible for every crime that takes place in this country."

Hear that? It's the world's smallest violin playing outside of a small illegitimate Italian deli just for you.

"You'd think I had unlimited power and a swell pocketbook. Well, I guess I got the power all right; but the bank book suffers from these hard times as much as anyone else's. My pay roll is about as big as it ever was, but the profits have done their share of dwindling. Say, you'd be surprised if you knew some of the fellas I've got to take care of."

This is arguably the first humblebrag designed to throw the FBI and IRS off someone's scent.

(If any of Capone's grandchildren are reading this, please don't murder me.)

Adolf Hitler

"I die with a joyful heart in the awareness of the immeasurable deeds and achievements of our soldiers at the front, of our women at home, the achievements of our peasants and workers, and the contribution, unique in history, of our youth, which bears my name."—from Hitler's suicide note, April 29, 1945

Is there any more humble a brag than humblebragging on one's suicide note? Take that, Hitler! I am gently ribbing you in a cheap Urban Outfitters book. Justice is served!

George Bernard Shaw

Keeping things on the old-school tip, here's a classic one from famous playwright, G. B. Shaw.

"I have not succeeded: people have agreed to rank me as successful: that is all. Have I not written somewhere that life levels all men: death reveals the eminent."

The ol' "yeah I'm successful, but death reveals the eminent" humblebrag. He's a great playwright, so it makes all the sense in the world that his humblebrags would hold the same poetic wit. Also, he totally called this one: He is now very dead.

Marilyn Monroe

Marilyn Monroe was the Joe DiMaggio of humblebrags and marrying multiple people including Joe DiMaggio.

> "I'm selfish, impatient and a little insecure. But if you can't handle me at my worst, then you sure as hell don't deserve me at my best."

Well, well. Someone thinks they're the bee's knees.

Sammy Davis Jr.

What do you think when you think Sammy Davis Jr.? How ugly he is? No, right? Well, that's apparently what he thinks.

> "[God] gave me this extraordinary wife, so good, so beautiful. And he not only granted that I should love her but also that she should love me, ugly as I am, with only one eye, and a broken nose, and small too..."

See? He's like an insecure hot high school girl.

"Complete ugliness, utter ugliness, like mine, though, is almost attractive."

I truly had no idea that Sammy Davis Jr. thought he was so ugly. This is just kind of sad now. He seemed to have so much confidence! Chin up, babe!

Johnny Ramone

"I don't need much more money, and I thought that when I retired that nobody would want to talk to me anymore. Then I did, and people still want to talk to me."

Thank God he didn't need more money. (By this I am implying that I'm glad he retired because his music was not good. I'm sorry, it wasn't. Great T-shirts though!)

Kurt Cobain

I like Nirvana a lot and I remember as a kid always thinking that Kurt Cobain was super "real," whatever "real" means to a ten year old. Integrity aside, even Kurt was not immune from humblebraggery.

"The thrill and embarrassment of becoming international pop stars was too much, so we opened our mouths and put our foot in sometimes."

It seems a little tasteless to include this Kurt quote knowing just how "too much" becoming a pop star was for him, but nonetheless this was a humblebrag.

"I may not be well read, but when I do read, I read well."

I like this one because it's from his own journal, which means he humblebragged to himself.

"I spent all of my life trying to stay away from sports and here I am in a sporting arena."

On stage in front of tens of thousands adoring fans. Sucks dude.

"I can't play [guitar] like Segovia. The flip side of that is that Segovia could probably never have played like me."

You hear him, Andres Segovia??! You got nuthin' on Cobain!

Madonna

"A lot of people are just really confused by me…
Maybe they just feel unsafe. But any time you have an

overtly emotional or irrational, negative reaction to something, you're fearing something that it's bringing up in you."

Is it that hard to believe that some people may just actually not like you, Madonna? What am I saying—of course it is.

Mort Sahl

Mort Sahl is a comedian and the oldest living human being. He has written jokes about every major war since the French Revolution.

"I mean, how do you explain the fact—everybody in the United States knows me, and I'm not on television or in pictures. What put me on the cover of *Time*? Because *I had an audience. The audience* made me a hero."

My grandma says crazy stuff, too, sometimes, so I get it.

Pete Townshend

Pete Townshend is the lead child pornography researcher for The Who.

"The Who are rapidly becoming a circus act, one of those who always get good reviews...because they are simply going through the motions. We do what we've always done, it's good in its way, but it's like a good circus act."

A Piccadilly *Circus act. Get it? 'Cause they're British?*

Biggie Smalls

Most rap music falls somewhere on the scale of brag to humblebrag, so I don't know why I'm picking on Biggie. Maybe because he can't retaliate against me. I'm slowly realizing most of the people in this chapter are dead. And quickly realizing what a pussy I am.

"Mo' money, mo' problems."

Pretty quintessential humblebrag here. This is a foundational building block for future humblebragging and he did it in so few words.

Barack Obama

Obama's inaugural address contained some flagrant humblebragging right out of the gate. Here is the first line:

"I stand here today humbled by the task before us, grateful for the trust you have bestowed, mindful of the sacrifices borne by our ancestors."

Ba-rag Obama. Oh wait wait, Ba-rag O-blah-ma. There it is. Nicely done, Wittels. Thanks, me.

Ugh, Can You Believe They Included Me on This List?

Getting back to Twitter though, it seems like it's a natural desire to want to be ranked and ranked highly. Our urge for competition has existed since monkey times. It's the entire basis of sports and also of our entire way of life. People like knowing they are better than others at something. This section is devoted to humblebrags by people who are excited to have been selected for a variety of "lists"—some lamer than others.

Chris Anderson (@TEDchris)
Great choices at 1 and 3. 2 is surely a mistake! The Top 10 Good Men of 2010

I bet I can guess without even looking at this list, that Chris Anderson HIMSELF is number two . . . (I didn't include the list in the book, but I was right. He was number two).

🐗 🐗 🐗

Cary Brothers (@carybrothers)
oddly i have music in the itunes top 40 singer-songwriter,

dance, and soundtrack categories. thank you, 2011. all proceeds will go to pizza.

It's odd in that I've never heard of you. I love pizza, though, so keep it up!

Kanye West (@kanyewest)
I was actually surprised that a record as raw as H*A*M could make it to #2 on Itunes.

No you weren't, Kanye. You're Kanye. Your whole thing is over-confidence, remember?

Adam Carolla (@adamcarolla)
Just made #1 on iTunes audiobooks. Thanks you guys.
Check it out before it gets crowned by Snookie or the Kardashians.

The sad part of this humblebrag is that I think his book actually did get knocked out by Snooki's book.

Mike Doughty (@Mike_Doughty_)
Learned that a song of mine charted at no. 38 in

Billboard--legit top 40! Always envied one-hit-wonders, thinking I'm a no-hit-wonder.

Aw, chin up and yes.

John Moe (@johnmoe)
· The fact that Wikipedia lists me as a notable alumnus of my college speaks ill of the reliability of crowd sourced information.

Pssst, John. Hey, John. Psst. Did you edit that Wikipedia page? You can tell me. It's just us.

Joe Posnanski (@JPosnanski)
Impossible as this is to believe, this is the No. 1 sports podcast on iTunes at the moment.

Why is that impossible to believe? You're a guy with a very popular sports podcast. So popular that it's number one in fact.

Jen Royle (@Jen_Royle)
If the folks who voted me into Balt Mags most eligible bachelors saw me walkin the pup right now they'd quickly remove me from list #Fact

For walking a dog? What kind of animal-hating magazine is this?!?

Mike Tyson (@MikeTyson)
I heard I am the 2nd most influential athlete on Twitter &
Facebook.. not bad for a guy who a year ago, didn't know
what social media was!

And who nineteen years ago was raping someone!

Brittany Snow (@Brittanysnow)
Ok @MaximMag, what the hell were yall drinkin when u
made this list of urs? Even being mentioned w/ these girls
is crazy Thank U

*They were thinking that you have a nice body. You've been the lead
in a lot of movies. You must have started to put together by now that
you are attractive, right?*

Rob Thomas (@ThisIsRobThomas)
thanx to billboard for naming me the #5 songwriter of
the decade. i think your math is probably wrong, but i'll
take it.

Are you saying you should've been number one? Be happy with five, Matchbox!

♨ ♨ ♨

Kevin Goldstein (@Kevin_Goldstein)
Apple's iTunes rankings confuse me, as we're suddenly at an all time high by a MILE. No. 3 sports podcast PERIOD. #Thanks #Really?

You seem to have a pretty firm grasp on it. Pretty standard list shit.

♨ ♨ ♨

Ken Jennings (@KenJennings)
Hey, if you put me in your /celebs list, I'm flattered, but let's be honest: that's the most expansive definition of "celeb" possible.

Oof boy, a lot to be bothered by here. Firstly, Ken Jennings is quite literally a know-it-all. He won Jeopardy! *seven thousand times. He knows every piece of information. So, off the bat, I find him annoying. But for such a smart guy, you'd think he'd know the definition of a word as elementary as "celebrity." Even I know that one, and I've only won* Jeopardy! *three times. Jennings is definitely a celebrity. He holds a title on one of the longest running TV shows in the world. Lastly, you can't use the phrase "let's be honest" and then not be honest.*

Ugh, I Can't Believe I Won an Award/Ugh, I Can't Believe I'm at This Awards Show

Being nominated for an award or being at an awards show is like getting to be on a list in front of an audience! The fact that they carry such a cultural cache makes it seem completely okay to brag about it, but it isn't. When you buy a gun, you have to wait five days so they make sure you are of sane mind. I think the same grace period should apply to attendees of awards shows. You shouldn't be allowed to tweet or text about it for the five days before and after. Nothing in Hollywood brings out the humblebrag in people quite like an awards show. This doesn't exclusively happen in Hollywood, but it is there that it gets taken to some next-level shit.

Alexa Chung (@alexa_chung)
PS> Brian Ferry presented my award which feared me out because he's such an icon. #tonguetied

Oh yeah? Well, if he's such an icon, then why did I have to Google him??? (FULL DISCLOSURE: After Googling him, I came to learn that he is actually an icon, but still . . .)

Mark Ronson (@iamMarkRonson)
extremely grateful for my brit nomination. having seen
the other nominees, there is no way in hell that I'm
winning, but psyched nonetheless

This seems to be the only manner in which people accept a nomination for something. I'd love to see someone change the game on this. "I'm the best person nominated for this and I should win it." That would be baller!

          🐦 🐦 🐦

Michael Georgoff (@mtgeorgoff)
Critic's Choice Movie Awards! Seated on the main
floor. They got confused and mixed us up with real
celebs. Oops.

Oops, you said "oops."

          🐦 🐦 🐦

Nathan Fillion (@NathanFillion)
Wow. All done at Emmys. It was an honor just to be
nominated. Oh. Wait. Rats.

You can sour grapes all you want, but you're still on a TV show and you still went to the Emmys.

RainnWilson (@rainnwilson)
So glad the awards season lines up with the cold and flu
season. #sickattheSAGawards

DayQuil, dawg! Best of luck.

Kim Kardashian (@KimKardashian)
I'm freaking out! Having a fashion emergency with my
Grammy dress! KaufmanFranco came to my rescue!!!

I'm guessing the emergency is that it won't fit over your ass?
*   Also, I don't know who Kaufman Franco is, but I presume that
was some sort of name-drop.*

Lucian Walker (@GodsPaparazzi)
grammy party nite 2, i really dont wanna drink tonight !!!
dammit hahahaha

Where I come from, you laugh hysterically after a joke.

andy barron (@andybarron)
rumor has it my hello hurricane book for @switchfoot is

up for a dove award. i didn't know my mom voted for dove awards. thanks!

You're implying that only one person votes on the Dove Awards, meaning it's not a legitimate award. Way to bite the hand that feeds ya, pal! Also when you say "Dove," we talking chocolate or soap? Is that the same company? Now this is just an irrelevant tangent I've gone on.

Dusty Trice (@DustyTrice)
Because I'm a Shorty Awards finalist my name is showing up on all of these @SelenaGomez and @JustinBieber fan sites. I totally get it now.

Get what?

Neil Patrick Harris (@ActuallyNPH)
Happy Oscar Sunday! I'm grateful that I'll be watching from my living room this year, and not hyperventilating offstage, about to perform.

We get it. You hosted the Oscars. Let it go.

Lena Dunham (@lenadunham)
Q: what felt better, winning a #SpiritAward or removing those spanx? A: BOTH FELT AMAZING.

You didn't let me guess!

Alex Sagalchik (@AlexSagz)
Tim Burton sightings always give me the chills. It's all
about the Weinstein Bash. #Oscars

*I think I speak for everyone when I say how-the-fuck-often do you
have a Tim Burton sighting?*

moby (@thelittleidiot)
my friends think it's strange to bring a sandwich to the
oscars. i mean, 5 hours in kodak theater? I'll get hungry.
thus: sandwich.

*What's the over/under on how many times Moby told somebody
"I'm sneaking a sandwich into the Oscars" followed by a coy smile?
Fifty times? A hundred? Guh.*

Skrillex (@Skrillex)
About to walk this red carpet at the Woodies...Nervous
as F*CK

*Skrillex is a fourteen-year-old dubstep DJ who—as far as I can tell—
is known for his half-shaved head and ambiguous acne. Apparently he*

was nervous about the Woodies, which seems silly. It's the Woodies. I'm not even sure Skrillex knows what the Woodies are. I'm not even sure the Woodies know what the Woodies are.

Pat Healy (@Pat_Healy)
Really enjoy looking at pictures of myself on red carpets. AKA 'Guy Who Doesn't Know What To Do With His Hands Slideshow.'

I like Pat Healy and I like the humor of this, but it's still a humblebrag.

Carolyn Fell (@CarolynFell)
I just stepped on gum. Who spits gum on a red carpet?

Maybe Brad Pitt?!? Could have been Pattinson!! AhhhhHHHH-HHHH!!!!!! Yayyyyy!!!!

Amir Khan (@AmirKingKhan)
Haha who saw me on national soap awards I didn't no it was on till I saw me on tv. Embarrassing moment lol

What the shit are you talking about?

Georgia Frances King (@georgiafrancesk)
Just got told that I won another RMIT journalism award
again… Cheap champagne and cheese squares here
I come!

If you didn't give a shit about it, you wouldn't have tweeted it. Come on, lady. It's also clear how much Georgia wanted us to know this wasn't her first RMIT journalism award. With words like "another" and "again." For her, it's old hat! Old unremarkable hat! Old unremarkable hat that she remarked on!

Neil Diamond (@NeilDiamond)
I googled "icon", it's a small computer graphic. Yep, that
sounds about right. Thanks, Billboard, for the Icon Award
and the love! Neil

Sometimes when old rock stars make jokes, they SOUND like jokes, but if you inspect them closely they're nonsense. Probably from all the acid and heroin. This may or may not be an example of that, but it's definitely an example of a type of humblebrag.

Steven Moffat (@steven_moffat)
20 years ago, I watched myself on telly winning a BAFTA.
Thought I looked quite handsome. Just watched last
night's. Oh. Dear. God.

*Didn't really need that whole preamble, or the . . . post-amble? I don't
know what you call it. The amble? Anyway, none of this needed to
be said.*

⁂

Tara Palmeri (@tarapalmeri)
I'm on a red carpet that is flooding and just lost power –
to brave it or go inside…

Just tweet about it.

⁂

Cage The Elephant (@CageTheElephant)
Dang, got a VMA nomination, we fooled those idiots!
Congrats to Manchester orchestra and black keys and foo
fighters also!

*Pretty textbook humblebrag stuff here. Probably not good to call the
people giving you an award "idiots," but I suppose you had to throw
in some humble one way or another. (Also, I actually liked their
album and hope they won. Don't care enough to find out.)*

⁂

Pauley Perrette (@PauleyP)
AGH! Awful moment when in PJ's chilling with dogs &
working on music & realize you have to be on a Red
Carpet in an hour!

Oh, you mean that awful moment when everything in life is great and you are dying to tell everyone about it?

🐷 🐷 🐷

Peter Jones (@dragonjones)
At the national Reality TV awards. You're not going to believe it (I don't yet) but just won Celebrity Personality of the Year! #cantberight

The lady (guy) doth protest too much!

🐷 🐷 🐷

Homer J. Simpson (@HomerJSimpson)
I'm nominated for a #TeenChoiceAward! Til now the only thing teens have chosen me for is to ask me to buy them beer.

People gave me a lot of shit for retweeting a humblebrag from Homer Simpson. But being animated doesn't exempt you from humblebragging. Sorry, Homie!

🐷 🐷 🐷

Ken Levine (@KenLevine)
Son's wedding day. It will be nice putting on a tuxedo and not losing an Emmy.

Way to use your son's wedding day as an excuse to talk about all the Emmys you've been nominated for.

Ugh, I'm "Genuinely" Asking!

This is one of my favorite forms of humblebragging. It isn't "self-effacing" in the standard humblebrag way, but it's still humble in that the offender is pretending to be unaware of something. But in the age of the Internet, the only person you need to ask any of this shit to is Google. Sometimes it's people asking for something easily Google-able, but sometimes it's people "genuinely" asking for people's opinions on things; things like a title for their new TV show or advice on something cool they are privileged enough to do. It's basically just fishing for compliments on a mass level. And it sucks.

Tyra Banks (@tyrabanks)
Ouch! I think I'm developing carpel tunnel from writing MODELLAND novel.Plus I type with 3-4 fingers.Besides typing lessons, any remedies?

Don't give models book deals?

Stephanie Wei (@StephanieWei)
A tad annoyed to find that housekeeping broke my phone

charger. Anyone staying in Kapalua got a spare? Don't have a car to drive to store.

Oh come on. You know damn well no one is staying in Kapalua.

Billy Dec (@BillyDec)
Just offered private jet ride home 5a. Do I pull that all nighter & feel awkward for a couple days, or go regular tmrw? Help!

Sorry I got to this too late. Hopefully you figured out your jet quandary and everything turned out all good!

mark schlereth (@markschlereth)
Need a new title for my new sitcom. CBS didn't like Home game. How bout some help?

I don't think they liked whatever he ended up going with. This show did not happen.

Shandi Finnessey (@ShandiFinnessey)
Anyone got a pic of the 2 Women's World magazines I was on the cover of? Long story but you'd be a huge help if you could send them to me…

In the running for potentially the most boring story on the planet: how supermodel, Shandi Finnessey, doesn't own the two Woman's World *magazines she was on the covers of.*

🐷 🐷 🐷

Judalina Neira (@TheJudalina)
Polling the Actors Out there: Do you take your manager with you to agent meetings?

You should definitely *take your PR person, so you don't say stuff like this anymore.*

🐷 🐷 🐷

Sophie Dee (@sophiedee)
I forget. What airport do u fly into to get to Maui?

I think you fly into Google-It International.

Ugh, I'm So Successful

Perceived success at something is really the foundation of all humblebrags, but these are specifically job-related ones. Any person who's ever had a job has probably committed a humblebrag at one time. Let's say you were a data processor and you tweeted something like, "I finished processing all my data too quickly and now I'm bored :(," you might end up on the humblebrag feed. Or let's say you were a guy who sells crabs to Thai restaurants (perhaps overly specific, but go with me here). If you tweeted something like, "Argh, I sold out of all my crabs! Now I have no crabs left to sell!" you might get retweeted by the humblebrag feed. That being said, the majority of these are still entertainment industry related, because they are the worst.

Darren Criss (@DarrenCriss) Woah...a wild feeling to sit alone in an empty diner and know you've got a song chillin as the #1 single on iTunes

I think the "wild feeling" you're referring to is probably more about the song on iTunes than the part about being alone in a diner. In

fact, being alone in a diner is perhaps the least wild event that could happen to a person.

🐷 🐷 🐷

christine teigen (@chrissyteigen)
so many big meetings, on hold for an amazing job, and the fucking snow is fucking it all the fuck up. fuck fuck fuck

Language!

🐷 🐷 🐷

perou (@mrperou)
ARRRRGH FML. now I've got a justin bieber shoot i can't do because I'm already shooting: what's with these clashes? grrr

Hey. HEY! Take it easy, photographer! Let's just all calm down and stop growling for one minute! Are you chilled out? Okay then, listen up: Who gives a shit.

🐷 🐷 🐷

Myles N. Miller (@mylesnmiller)
House Press Elevator is slow!

Wait, but the only people who gain access to the White House press elevator are—ohhhhhh, okay I see now. Well done, Myles.

Scott Mescudi (@wizardcud)
just realized something. i hve not received a plaque for
the double platinum plus sales of Day n Nite nor for the
Gold success of MOTM1

Those plaque-hoarding bastards will not get away with this. Don't
worry, Kid Cudi. Unacceptable. This is unacceptable.

Nick Barnett (@NickBarnett)
Only thing that sucks about being in super bowl is we
won't be able to see all the great commercials lol

YouTube them the next day, my dude! There. Now you can be 100
percent stoked on being in the Super Bowl.

Matt Jones (@mattjonesisdead)
On set for 12 hours. Thank God this show is amazing.
I'm a lucky fucker

I think the jury's still out on if it's okay to call your own show
"amazing." Okay, they're back; it isn't.

Josh Radon (@Yoshifett_BRB)
I just received an award for my teaching!?!?

#whaaaaaaa? #thedangersofpublicschools
#theawardisliterallyabaleofhay

Teachers are by and large the kindest group of people that exist. There are evil/terrible ones sure, but on the whole they enrich the lives of children for little reward. So, this is what happens when you reward them.

🐏 🐏 🐏

Whitney Hess (@whitneyhess)
Being in demand means disappointing 95% of people 95% of the time. I have yet to learn how to overcome this.

You can start by not being so gosh darn in demand! (Also, who are you?)

🐏 🐏 🐏

Timothy Burke (@bubbaprog)
Having the #1 video on YouTube is more hassle (i.e. dumbass comments & 1,500 emails in 24 hours) than it's worth (which is nothing).

So quit makin' such great dang vids!

🐏 🐏 🐏

jona weinhofen (@jonaweinhofen)
I love arriving at the 'party' & realizing they conveniently

left off the words 'press & interview' before the word
'party'

I don't get it. So now . . . you have to interview people? Who are you?

Meghan O'Keefe (@megsokay)
Should I be concerned that everyone in NYC comedy
seems to have my personal email (& uses it to ask for
press) or is it a sign of success?

I think you know the answer to this. (Neither.)

Ashley Greene (@AshleyMGreene)
Guess I better get used to early morning set calls :) good-
morning everyone!

Let's not make this an every morning thing.

Thomas Dale (@ThomasDale5)
My pen literally jus ran out of ink . . . thats how much
writing i have to do for this MTV thing. My fuckin hand
and brain hurt.

*Try switching to a computer. Or even typewriter. Did you tweet this
in 1512?*

Brad McLaughlin (@Brad_McLaughlin)
So now begins the task of sifting through 40 hours of
footage. #imaproducernow

*I don't think that's what a producer does. Sounds like you may be
an assistant editor now?*

🐷 🐷 🐷

Josh Freese (@joshfreese)
Eating at Phoenix airport and being tortured by having 2
listen 2 a hugely successful song I play on but cant stand
#servesmeright

*Josh Freese plays in Weezer now. Is it a Weezer song? It's gotta be
a Weezer song, right? It must.*

🐷 🐷 🐷

Robby Starbuck (@robbystarbuck)
I don't care if I have a 2 day long migraine from hell I will
finish the smashing pumpkins edit tonight or you can
meet me in hell! :)

This guy's obsessed with hell!

🐷 🐷 🐷

Caleb Lovely (@Caleblovely)
I just got a voicemail from LA. It was American idol

asking me to audition. #ifihadanickeleverytime
#forgetaboutIt #truth #getoffmysack

I'd be willing to bet you wouldn't have that many nickels, if any.

Shandi Finnessey (@ShandiMissUSA)
Reading the contracts for my new shows is like trying to
read Latin. Or Martian. Or the King James version of the
Bible. ;) Takes time...

*I'm gonna bet that for **@ShandiMissUSA**, reading anything is like
trying to read Latin or Martian.*

Kevin Hart (@KevinHart4real)
I'm watching the UCLA & FLORIDA game in amazement
because I performed in the same arena where they are
playing now & sold out #GodisGood

*Hey, let's not make this about you, eh? Also, if God is real and we
have the same one, and a big priority for him is making sure you sell
out a show at a college basketball arena, then I want out.*

Ali Cobrin (@AliCobrin)
Tested for 3 pilots in the past 3 weeks and the

consolation prize was the flu but now I'm healthy and
better than ever!

This was the worst story I've ever heard.

🐷 🐷 🐷

Anne V (@AnneV)
From the airport straight to the set - its hard to be major!
But I feel so blessed for it!

Sounds easy enough. You just went from one location to another
place. Let's leave God out of this.

🐷 🐷 🐷

Charles Melton (@_MELTON_)
6 Effin shoots next week.........ugh. good to finally work

Wait, so are you bothered or not? Make up your mind, Melton.

🐷 🐷 🐷

Frankie James Grande (@FrankieJGrande)
Just trying to wrap my head around the fact that my
Broadway show is opening tomorrow...Gulp.

It's complex stuff. Try not to overthink it.

Coco Rocha (@cocorocha)
Just randomly saw myself on the cover of March Elle Czech.
I guess no one tells me these things anymore. Děkuji!

You didn't put it together when you were at the cover shoot for it?

Robert Florence (@robertflorence)
Out with a personal trainer tomorrow as I begin to
transform myself for a "part" in a "thing". Ugh. Wish me
luck. Machinist territory.

The quotation marks did not help douche this down. Sorry, dude.

George Dohrmann (@georgedohrmann)
Exclusive: Pulitzer Prize winner filing expense reports on
a Saturday night. #excitinglife

*You know it's not, like, "a thing" that Pulitzer Prize winners don't
file expense reports, right?*

Michael Malone (@MaloneComedy)
My voice keeps going in and out.. No biggie just have two
sold out shows to do where I talk for an hour #FML

You tooootally could have left out the "sold out" part. But you didn't
and now here we are.

Dustin Pari (@dustinpari)
After all these years I am still not accustomed to seeing
my name up on signs around town.

Which town? I've seen zero.

Bryan A. Garner (@BryanAGarner)
Today: the second time in my life to make page one of the
NYT. No doubt the last!

What's sad about this is that Bryan Garner is a reporter for the
New York Times. *(Naw, I'm just playin'. I don't know.)*

Brendan Bradley (@brendanAbradley)
I'm shooting two commercials today…and
somehow I still don't have a commercial agent
#keepingmy10%

Yeah, you tell 'em! JK, don't tell anyone that.

Stewart Cink (@stewartcink)
I need to clean out my travel backpack more often. Just found my Masters player badge from 2006 in there.

Heh.

Lolo Jones (@followlolo)
hey can someone order a pizza for me? an Olympic athlete ordering a Large pizza for themselves is like a pastor going to a liquor store

I'm not sure if this is a knock on pizza guys or on Lolo Jones, but I'm not sure how many pizza guys have heard of Lolo Jones.

Pauley Perrette (@PauleyP)
It's so...so...??? every time you read articles about yourself & the facts are all wrong So strange, but, whatever :)

You don't have to type your inner monologue exactly how it is in your head.

demarcus cousins (@boogiecousins)
Watching the draft...I'm nervous like I'm getting drafted again!

Ugh, fine, I'll say it: Congrats on having been drafted!

Taylor Swift (@taylorswift13)
In my dressing room getting ready to play Gillette
Stadium tonight. I can't for the life of me believe that
we're playing here tomorrow too.

Where's Kanye when ya need him?

Brandon Sanderson (@BrandSanderson)
Well, now I feel important. They sent a limo for me. Feels
very…empty. I need some roadies or something in here
with me.

Awwwww (ful).

Counting Crows (@countingcrows)
Seriously? 2 headlines in 1 day? Only me. I should enter
a contest.

Only *you? You mean* Somehow *you, Counting Crows.*

50 Cent (@50cent)
Man I think I made a bad investment. I put to much energy into a women. I lose again but I'm doing great in business.

I actually take comfort in knowing that even 50 Cent has girl woes. Still had to include this though, on account of that ending.

Greg Olsen (@gregolsen82)
Walking into sports authority buying own jersey an awkward experience. At least they had quench gum

Your team probably provides those, ya know.

Alec Baldwin (@AlecBaldwin)
It's Rome. It's Woody. I still wanna sleep till at least nine. Show biz. F*%# me.

Some people have to wake up at five to clean urinals.

Ugh, I'm a Genius

Smart people *looooove* to humblebrag, which isn't that surprising. Most of the smart people I know are socially awkward, so it makes sense for them to excel at humblebragging. And what I love about smart people humblebragging is that they sound dumb doing it. It conveys a certain degree of unawareness. So, without further ado: Nerds.

Andy Borowitz (@BorowitzReport)
A major university just asked me to mentor journalism students. I had to explain my role: I'm part of the problem.

You must've known that including the word "major" makes that sound kind of braggy, right?

Alfredo (@NOLA_Fredo)
You know what sucks? Being TOO qualified for most jobs. WTF? Since when did being smart, competent or capable count against you?

I like pretending that this was written after an interview at a Chick-fil-A.

Trenni Kusnierek (@trenni)
For the 3rd time in 3 yrs I've been asked to speak at Harvard, but I've yet to speak at my alma mater. What's a girl gotta do @MarquetteU?

Just gotta tweet it probably.

Sentletse (@Sentletse)
So the International Journal of Genetics and Molecular Biology asks me to submit a paper. Do they know I'm a primary school drop-out!

Primary school? Like fifth grade? That's crazy, yo.

Stuart Ellman (@bikenyc)
I am giving the keynote speech at the columbia venture capital and private equity conference tomorrow. Actually, I am a bit fearful of it.

Sounds boring!

Annie Duke (@AnnieDuke)
Can we start a media campaign to question how I got into Columbia, too? Still scratching my head about how I got accepted & demand answers!

Yeah, fuck it, why not. Let's fire up that media campaign. Seems like news enough.

Steel Fontana (@CriticalA)
How is it that I graduated from law school and passed two bar exams, but I can't figure out how to properly load a dishwasher?

I dunno. I know stupid lawyers.

The Follower (@thefoll0wer)
Wow, just got an email asking me to apply to MIT for my MBA...I have 0 chance of getting in, but it sure is nice to get solicited.

Seems like you have a foot up on all the people not asked to apply. So there's that.

Micah Redding (@micahtredding)
Oh yeah, I got elected to Mensa's local executive committee. Not sure what that means.

C'monnnnnn, you know what that means.

ad contrarian (@AdContrarian)
Speaking at Stanford today. Funny that I'm smart enough to be a teacher there but not smart enough to be a student.

Not like "ha-ha" funny, but also not any other kind of funny.

Uh-oh, I'm on TV!

The TV industry is largely a place where people go to prove to their parents and middle school bullies that they are special. So, it comes as no surprise that they supply us with ample amounts of humblebragging. The humility is all bullshit, though. If you decide to come out to Hollywood to be in front of the camera, then clearly you think you deserve to be in front of the camera. You ain't foolin' nobody. Quit frontin', actors!

Olivia Wilde (@oliviawilde)
Dear Regis and Kelly audience, pls excuse my inevitable spew of incoherent, lazy eyed musings due to my current state of still awakeness.

This actually would have been a genuine apology if your only Twitter followers were the audience from Live *with Regis and Kelly. But, those are crazy odds.*

🐷 🐷 🐷

Russell Brand (@rustyrockets)
Watching self on Larry King. Achievement diminished in ad break by catheter commercial.

Achievement diminished by Arthur remake.

Russell Kane (@russell_kane)
Just watching my first ever TV stand-up set. Horrific moments of self loathing.

I don't even know what to say about this one. Just textbook stuff.

Holly MacKenzie (@stackmack)
Yuck. Hearing my voice on Raptors TV on NBATV. It's still deeper than normal from this stupid cough even though the cold is finally gone.

If it starts with "yuck" and has "TV" in it twice, it's probably a humblebrag.

Christopher Hayes (@chrislhayes)
Really looking forward to *watching* rather than *hosting* @maddow tonight. The former is a million times easier. (at least)

Subtext: Did everyone see me host Maddow? Please let me host Maddow again.

Teresa Strasser (@teresastrasser)
"@TheTalk_CBS: #THETALK delivered its largest weekly audience ratings ever" I'm on today to cool off hot streak

So, THAT'S what you were leading up to! I was all, "take it easy with The Talk *stats." But, okay, I see where you were heading with it now.*

Kai Ryssdal (@kairyssdal)
The CNN-LA green room is a cold and lonely place at 7 on a Sunday morning.

I would be remiss to not show the tweet he paired this one with. They are a package deal if you ask me . . .

Funnily enough, CNN LA green room a cold and lonely place at 10 on a Monday too.

Sadly, Kai left us all hanging as to what a CNN LA greenroom is like at 1 in the afternoon on a Tuesday. And now, we'll never know. Though, it seems like it's safe to assume that it's a cold and lonely place at that time as well.

Blake Williger (@BlakeAndProud)
I'm on the series finale of "Hannah Montana" tonight. Watch the Golden Globes instead.

You, my friend, have got yourself a deal!

Tony Robbins (@tonyrobbins)
My tv partners got me to agree to revisit QVC-It's 6:45 am
est -on in 15 min-what was I thinking?! LOL call me 800-
395-1601 share your story

*If you were actually a good motivational speaker, I would have
watched this.*

John Berman (@johnsberman)
Someone has made a terrible mistake. I am anchoring @
abcworldnews on Sunday. One night only, as they say in
"Dreamgirls."

*Dreamgirls didn't invent "one night only." Yeah, that's what I'm
choosing to take you to task on instead of humblebragging.*

Tokyo Police Club (@TokyoPoliceClub)
You know you've made it when Ron MacLean gets your
band name wrong on national TV...

What's sad is that Tokyo Police Club went on to not make it.

Charlie Sheen (@charliesheen)
Just got invited to do the Nancy Grace show...I'd rather go on a long road trip with Chuck Lorre in a '75 Pacer...

Here's a humblebrag by Charlie Sheen. Hopefully Charlie Sheen didn't die by the time this book came out.

Danny Forster (@dannyforster)
I'm watching myself on TV right now (which is just an odd experience in and of itself) and I'm taken aback by how much I'm sweating—in HD

Man you squeezed an incredible amount of humblebrag into 140 characters.

Metric (@Metric)
SO happy I didn't wipe out on the icy stage in front of millions of viewers.

Not sure what event Metric is talking about, but I'm glad I didn't tune in. They didn't even fall down. I don't wanna see the band Metric not fall down.

Dan Harmon (@danharmon)
They're celebrating St. Paddy's at NBC. Crazy drunks

picked us up for a 3rd season. Thank you, NBC and all
our viewers.

Sometimes on Twitter, people will take issue with some of the hum-
blebrags I choose for the feed, arguing that they aren't truly humble-
brags. And sometimes the person calling me out is Dan Harmon
(creator of NBC's Community*), and sometimes he is right! Any-*
way, this was a humblebrag. And, now Dan will probably argue that
it isn't. He may say that he was joking and that he doesn't actually
think that the executives at NBC were actually drunk. But, a self-
deprecating joke announcement of true good fortune constitutes as a
humblebrag in my book . . . which is this book.

Naughty But Nice Rob (@NaughtyNiceRob)
I can't get used to seeing my face on taxi tv! #STRANGE!
Especially when you are sitting with someone you just
met! What do you say?

Say what you said here. Point out that it's your face and then just
yell the word "STRANGE!" at him.

Christian Sprenger (@CASprenger)
After seven weeks of yummy on-set catering, I have
lost all technical ability to make myself breakfast
#viciouscycle

Better get on another project so you don't starve!

Michelle Bernstein (@chefmichy)
omg i hate watching #topchef when im on it! i never know
if ill come out like a schmuck

I didn't see that episode of Top Chef, *but I can tell you how you
came out here . . .*

🐷 🐷 🐷

Elizabeth A. Terrell (@EATerrell)
I love it when major news outlets post ridiculously bad
pictures of me online- really, I do . . . OY! How's YOUR
Friday going?! :)

Not just any news outlets, people. MAJOR ones.

🐷 🐷 🐷

Skylar Grey (@SkylarGrey)
Trying to get some sleep so that I'll be able to have a
coherent conversation with Carson Daly at 8am. I'm just
not tired. . . . grrr.

*Don't even worry about it. You could get fourteen hours of sleep and
would still have a hard time having a coherent conversation with
Carson Daly.*

🐷 🐷 🐷

Nick W-K (@NickWK)
"Hey! Gimme some of that biscotti man please!" - Me

(offscreen), on tonights 'The Hard Times of RJ Berger.' See you at the SAG awards.

Hey, man, some of us never got to ask R. J. Berger for some of his biscotti. Perspective, bro.

🐷 🐷 🐷

Kevin Smith (@ThatKevinSmith)
HOLLYWOOD! Do not adjust your television sets! That ugly image you'll be staring at on the @KTLAMorningNews around 9:20a.m. is ME! LOOOOK!!!

Translation for Kevin Smith's fans: Snoochie boochie, Snoogins (snong bong).

🐷 🐷 🐷

Bag Snob® (@BagSnob)
Watching my segment on FOX and cringing....Listening to my voice on tv is SO painful. Do I really sound like such a valley girl?!?!

It's not so much the voice as it is the whining.

🐷 🐷 🐷

David Hasselhoff (@DavidHasselhoff)
Its an evening with the Hoff! Britain's got talent followed by my life story on Piers Morgan. Hopefully you won't get sick of me!

They did :(

🐷 🐷 🐷

Minnie Gupta ♥✍ (@MinnieGupta)
Haven't watch TV in so long that when they called to
book me for "Conan" I imagined the Barbarian. Wanted
to wear a hot Amazon costume :(

*The booker pronounced Conan's name wrong? They should fire
that dude.*

🐷 🐷 🐷

Brian Moylan (@BrianJMoylan)
I'm on VH1 at 9:30. It's way too early to be on TV.

*Maybe, but it's not live is it? VH1 doesn't have a ton of live morn-
ing news programs to my knowledge. You probably already taped
this. So who cares what time you're on TV?*

🐷 🐷 🐷

Jared Loftus (@JaredLoftus)
The thing I heard the most last night? "Jared, seriously?
Shave before you go on national TV."

*That means you had a lot of conversations last night that started
with you telling someone that you were gonna be on national TV.
Sounds unbearable.*

Joshua Kaufman (@jmk)
If anyone captured any of the morning show video and
could send me a link, I'd really appreciate it! (I don't own
a TV or really watch TV.)

*For a guy who doesn't give a shit about TV, you certainly care a lot
about TV.*

Gabriel (@asigabeitweet)
Just got cast in another HBO show...HA! #notanactor

What are you, Gabriel?

Stephanie Wei (@StephanieWei)
Wait, what? I think I made a cameo on NBC. Crap, I knew
I should have blow dried my hair this morning!

Wait, whoa, HUH?!? HOLD UP? Whaaaaa!!?

Gabriel Rutledge (@gaberutledge)
Tomorrow TV taping. Saturday the Porterhouse
Steakhouse in Moses Lake WA. Not exactly how I thought
it would be when I started comedy.

You didn't think a life of comedy could include doing comedy and eating food? You're whatever the opposite of a psychic is.

🐷 🐷 🐷

Michael McKean (@MJMcKean)
Congrats to @KeithOlbermann on Countdown's ripping debut. I'll be on tonight to see if I can slow the momentum a tad. Cheers!

All right, real talk, dawg: How much of this was a sincere congratulations and how much was just a plug for you being in the show tonight?

🐷 🐷 🐷

Jonah Goldberg (@JonahNRO)
I'm in studio looking at monitor, man do I need a haircut.

You gotta get some mirrors for your house, man! That way you don't have to rely on acting gigs to gauge your hair length.

🐷 🐷 🐷

David Spade (@DavidSpade)
on leno this evening. watch me squirm around and mumble jokes. riveting tv. cancel all plans

I usually have a policy that if a humblebrag is done to promote something, then I try to not retweet it. People have to sell things and get people to show up to their concerts and see their movies and what not; I get it. But this one was too pitch-perfect of a humblebrag to leave out.

∗ ∗ ∗

Elin Hilderbrand (@elinhilderbrand)
Dear Good Morning, America: My name is Elin. Not Erin.
#petpeeve

You hear that, GOOD MORNING AMERICA?!? One more name blunder and you can kiss Erlin Happerdash good-bye!

∗ ∗ ∗

Brian Steinberg (@bristei)
How low can TV-news go? Local CBS station calls me to weigh in on the marketabilty of Casy Anthony. I declined

Thanks for keeping us posted on a thing that didn't happen.

∗ ∗ ∗

Atul Gawande (@Atul Gawande)
Talking about health care costs on MSNBC's Dylan Ratigan show at 4 pm EST (20 min), if anyone's really bored.

Or if anyone's not bored and would like to be.

Matt Davis (@LifeStageFilms)
Having phonecall today w/ the Associated Press/NBC's
Today Show. Wedding next week will be featured on TV,
but it's a nightmare. #notworthit

The wedding's not worth it? You need to tell her, man.

Rex Parker (@rexparker)
I'm going to need advice soon from someone who's been
on national television before. Topics: "what to wear" and
"how not to freak out"

Acid-washed overalls and Xanax.

Dara O Briain (@daraobriain)
Now, please God, let your telly be free of me for a while.
Oh shite, Mock the Week is still on...

*Gahhh, stop being so darn captivating and we wouldn't have to put
you on TV so darn much! Your fault!*

opie radio (@OpieRadio)
Hey @jimmyfallon TY for the invite to do tonights show.

Sorry I was unable to get back in time for the taping...so bummed. Let's do it soon.

Yo, Jimmy, me too. Sorry!

Austin Carr (@AustinCarr)
Note to self: Next time you're on CNN, don't look so angry.

Hey hey hey, let's not go around assuming we're gonna be on CNN again, okay?

Dianna Agron (@DiannaAgron)
I do find it strange to say....on my way to sit with David. Letterman.

Let's back it up. Are you a guest on his show? If so, not strange. If not, then okay.

Joe Magyer (@TMFInsideValue)
Taped my third TV spot on the debt ceiling in under 24 hours. At some point, someone will realize I only own one summery tie.

What's the over/under on how many people watched all three of
these TV spots? Let's put it at one.

Anjelah Johnson (@anjelahjohnson)
Thanx 4the love from everyl who watched my random
episode of Curb Your Enthusiasm last night. Totally 4got
about that, sorry no notice. #fb

Apology accepted, and thank you for the unnecessary post-notice,
letting us know you were on.

Buzz Bissinger (@buzzbissinger)
So anybody watch HBO Realsports last night? How
was I?

No. Don't know.

Abigail Maher (@Billymawa)
Just had my 'appearance on BBC1' cherry popped. I
looked like a pillock. Still, they can only work with what
they have! #Pointless

I think this woman is British. I don't know what a "pillock" is, but it sounds British. Could be a humblebrag, could not be. Once again, no clue what a pillock is.

David Krumholtz (@DaveKrumholtz)
I sincerely hope my new T.V. show does not get cancelled. That is all.

Dave, are you sitting down? It did.

Ugh, I Can't Believe I Was Mentioned in This Thing!

Question: How do you go about letting people know that you were mentioned in a newspaper or magazine? Well, here is how I think you do it: First—get mentioned in a newspaper or magazine. Then, whoever naturally reads said newspaper or magazine knows that you are in it and that should be enough. I'm not going to go pick up a *Corpus Christi Gazette* to see a picture of your church group hosting a bake sale on page C7. If I was meant to see it, I'd see it. Or, I guess you could do what these people did...

Michael Muhney (@michaelmuhney)
My dad was reading the paper this morning and handed this to me. Ha. Me and Keith Olbermann

Ha?

🐷 🐷 🐷

Rehan Jalali (@SixPackDietPlan)
The Washington Post called me "The sharpest young

tool in the nutritional shed" umm not sure how I feel bout being called a "tool"! Lol

Rehan, why do you always zero in on the bad stuff, bro? Accept that you are good enough, believe in yourself, and soar like an eagle!

🐌 🐌 🐌

Will Wilkinson (@willwilkinson)
Really wasn't expecting to be in New York mag and Boing Boing today.

Me neither. And I wasn't. Were you? I'm guessing you were.

🐌 🐌 🐌

Padma Lakshmi (@PadmaLakshmi)
Haha so when I tweeted on Sunday that I loved the new Newsweek I had no idea I was one of the 150 women mentioned! :)

So you said you loved it before you read it? Unethical! BUSTED!

🐌 🐌 🐌

Will Sturgeon (@sturgeo)
my picture was apparently in USA TODAY...today. i haven't read that paper...ever? but sweet!

I'll save you the time: that paper sucks, dude.

Ted Johnson (@WolvesCMO)
Enjoying the paper this morning only to find my own mug smiling back at me in the Sports section.Thankfully they only quoted the smart stuff

That was a real roller coaster. You liked it, then you saw your mug and didn't like it, then you liked it again!

Susan Orlean (@susanorlean)
My husband's comment on the story about me in today's NYTimes: "Oh, look! You're next to a story about Arnold Schwartzenegger!"

Oh, Arnold Schwarzenegger? You mean one of the biggest news stories of 2011? Sounds like a pretty good spot to be in news-wise.

Clay Shirky (@cshirky)
Undeserved but welcome: Guardian names Here Comes Everybody one of 100 best non-fiction books of all time

Oh yeah? Well, if it's so great then how come I haven't read it, huh? Is it because I've only read about five books from start to finish in my entire life, including Maniac Magee *in fifth grade and* Oliver Twist *in seventh grade? Huh, is that why? Oh, it is? Okay, cool. Well, then congrats on making the list... THE LIST OF HUMBLE-BRAGGERS! (No seriously, congrats on the list. I'm sorry for this one-sided confrontation.)*

Errol Morris (@errolmorris)
I'm not used to this sort of thing, but...I got a starred
review in Publishers Weekly

*Aren't used to what? Telling us about your accomplishments? It's
cool, just don't make a habit of it.*

Ugh, I'm at an Exclusive Event!

One of my favorite classifications of humblebrag. People *loooove* going to things that are exclusive, and unfortunately they *looove* telling people about it. A lot of red carpet and after-party action in this section. There is also a seemingly inordinate amount of people being scared of falling down at an inopportune moment. Why is this fear so rampant? Is it the fancy shoes? They're still just shoes. They are made for walking. I mean, how many times a day do you fall down? For me—it's zero. Though, these people seem to be faceplanting every forty seconds.

Chris Weingarten (@1000TimesYes)
Man, the talent pool at tonight's Da Capo reading was just formidable. Like all my favorite writers in one place. Touched to even be invited

So happy to not know what you're talking about.

🐷 🐷 🐷

Jaimie Alexander (@JaimieAlexander)
I have the largest bruise on my knee right now. I wore

really tall shoes to an event Thursday...and fell face
forward down stairs. #Classy

Oooooooooh, an event? What event? That's cool about the event!

Trevor Donovan (@TrevDon)
Invited to AMA after party, but instead of going there to
see Ke (dollar sign) ha...I'm going somewhere way more
fun...my BED...#Work early

Thanks for letting us know?

Lauren Waugh (@Laurenhwaugh)
Ugh I hate getting up at 430 but I guess going to the
playboy mansion isn't a bad reason to wake up

*Nothing like looking at some fake tits and Lou Ferrigno at the crack
of dawn. Oh wait, that sucks.*

Matt Dentler (@MattDentler)
Yes, I'm up early to see a film that opens in 11 days. But
it's "Tree of Life," and this is what Cannes is all about.

You hit the nail on the head. Cannes is literally about seeing films.

Guy Branum (@guybranum)
My movie premier is tonight. I'm sure I'll find some way to make this feel embarrassing or horrible.

You did it!

🐷 🐷 🐷

Carson Griffith (@CarsonGriffith)
Black Swan was amazing. The after party was almost just as disorienting and Natalie and Mila are awesome ppl. I rarely say that.

Let's chill on the whole "Natalie" and "Mila" thing. In general, I'd say that when someone refers to any celebrity by their first name alone, you can pretty much always bet that a humblebrag is soon to follow.

🐷 🐷 🐷

Brooklyn Decker (@BrooklynDDecker)
By the way. First and last time I will ever walk a red carpet in slippers I bought at Target. red carpet fail??? I think so.

Wait, WHAT color did you say the carpet was??

🐷 🐷 🐷

Daniel Dae Kim (@danieldaekim)
U know u're tired when u fall asleep getting ready 4 the

#H50 Xmas party. I guess saving someone from falling off a cliff will do that 2 u.

What's "pound sign H-fifty?" They got good Xmas parties?

⁂

Nicole Polizzi (@Sn00ki)
Damn sick mansion party! Huge lights and I forgot to wear white @ a white party. Just my luck. You here Ludacris?

Ya make it too easy, Snooks. Can I call you Snooks?

⁂

Matt Cherette (@mattchew03)
Oops—totally forgot about the "Skins" party tonight. I had a ~VIP~ invitation and everything, too.

Well, Skins *was canceled. I blame you.*

⁂

Carl Llaneta Rana (@CLRana9017)
Last night on line for SKINS party was probably more fun than the SKINS party itself. #justsaying.

Another Skins *party tweet? This* Skins *party had mad web presence, yo!*

Katy Stanchak (@katysavestheday)
The Skins party kept the VIP area humble last night by having port a potties in the dark. They thought this would keep the coke usage down.

Yet another one! Maybe if the Skins *crew spent a little more time on the show and a little less time throwing crazy ragers, it would be on the air today.*

🐗 🐗 🐗

dan nailen (@dannailen)
Hmm, a concert, a movie or a party? #sundanceishard

This made me laugh. I love when you don't know if it's a humble-brag or not until the hashtag at the end.

🐗 🐗 🐗

Rich Cimini (@RichCimini)
Just my luck: I'm in 3rd row of press box, can't see amazing scoreboard in middle of Cowboys Stadium. #SB45

I don't know a ton *about sports, so I can't really tell if there is some veiled esoteric sarcasm underneath this. But on the surface, this seems like a humblebrag.*

🐗 🐗 🐗

Everyl L♥vs Mamacita (@iamMAMACITA)
Last night I missed Kim Kardashian party

@RollingStoneLA. I was done off. So tired from last week and this weekend, I just couldn't do it

You WHAT?!??? How. Dare. You.

🐑 🐑 🐑

Peter Davis (@PeterDavisNYC)
Must only tweet nice things about stars as I'm going to Vanity Fair party soon - sweet celebrity karma: everyone looks amazing!!

Will you hurry up and attend this, so you go back to tweeting mean things about stars?! I need your celeb lambasts!

🐑 🐑 🐑

Cricket Lee (@crixlee)
JUST found out I was invited to Need For Speed party but I dunno if I can be ready and get there before midnight. Ahhhhhhhhhh

Crickets.

🐑 🐑 🐑

Kara Warner (@karawarner)
Highlight of Vanity Fair party thus far (in addition to chats w/ Judd Apatow, JJ Abrams, Anna Paquin) = free In 'N Out Burger for all!

If I'm being honest, I feel like you truly wanted us to focus on the stuff in the parentheses.

Guy Adams (@guyadams)
At the Oscar Governor's ball. Just spent 15 mins trying to find the cloakroom. Have now established that Americans call it the "coat check"

I bet you rounded that number up to fifteen so it would be worthy of mentioning.

Taryn Southern (@TarynSouthern)
Photos from tonight's @BattleLA premiere already up on my blog! I need to get better at getting candid party shots :P

That movie sucks!

Sheila Smith (@SheWhoTravels)
So, I got invited to go to the White House for an arts briefing next week. Hope I don't trip on a rug or do something stupid.

Odd fear.

Nylon Magazine (@NylonMag)
At the Strokes after party. Trying to look very hard like I
don't care. Not working.

Shouldn't have to work too hard. You're a magazine!

🐗 🐗 🐗

Zane Lamprey (@zanelamprey)
At Lakers Casino Night. Just lost all my chips to Ron
Artest. Hmph!

Reading this was more annoying than that time Ron Artest changed
his name to Metta World Peace.

🐗 🐗 🐗

Blue Velvet (@bluevelvetsfp)
Fuck! I just got offered a "free" artist pass to Coachella.
Between ppl becoming dead & becoming born, I can't go.
F you, cycle of life!

Why the quotation marks around "free"? Genuinely curious. Please
email me.

🐗 🐗 🐗

Lucy Yeomans (@LucyBAZAAR)
Panic for royal wedding outfit over. A happy encounter at

dinner last night with the uber chic designer L'wren Scott
and problem solved!

Don't care.

John Hodgman (@hodgman)
I regret I could not attend the Time 100 Gala last night,
but I was busy being hung by my ankles on the set of
BORED TO DEATH.

*Classic double brag. The self-deprecating thing here is about how he
was shooting a TV show.*

Ethan Smith (@ethanwsj)
Ever get busted sneaking out of a party embarrassingly
early? Ever run into Penelope Cruz while doing so?

Lemme guess. You have?

Alex Skolnick (@AlexSkolnick)
Tonight: private dinner/event by Miles Davis Estate- his
85th birthday w his family, musicians, media (Beyond
humbled/honored 2 b invited)

I wish Miles Davis were still alive, so that this tweet would have never happened.

Megan Ganz (@meganganz) VIP at the @wiredinsider party. Drinks by True Blood. Nerd alert!

I thought this was a humblebrag, but it turns out it's actually just a nerd alert. That's my bad.

Carolyn Kellogg (@paperhaus)
I am definitely not dressed well enough for a book party for an internationally-known designer. I'll NEVER be that well dressed.

Shush, ya look great, boo.

Amy & Nick (@karminmusic)
How the heck did we end up at the #ESPYS?! #thisiscrazy #SoSwag

I agree. How.

williambowerman (@williambowerman)
At the Armani party. I'm just here for the sandwiches.

Armani has the best sandwiches.

david carr (@carr2n)
Appearing at Hamptons Film Fest this weekend. 2nd
time have been to the Hamptons. Will singlehandedly up
#WhiteTrashDemo by my presence.

Can you tweet about being in the Hamptons twice and still be considered "white trash"? It's a paradox.

George Ruiz (@georgeruiz)
Just waved off the Super VIP couch within the VIP area of
this party. Hollywood you never fail to surprise, amuse.

What's that mean you waved it off? Like you were like, "Nahhh, I'm good, couch." I don't get it per se, but I know it's a humblebrag.

Um, How'd I Get Here???
How Is This My Life???

This is a somewhat common form of humblebragging. It's similar to the "Ugh, I'm at an Exclusive Event" humble-brag, except it's a step beyond. These people *reallllly* can't seem to even grasp how they are at wherever they are. They are downright flabbergasted. "How is this my life?" is a common expression among offenders of this humblebrag.

Jeremy Cowart (@jeremycowart)
Riding in a cornfield w/ strangers using an electronic device to watch @zacharylevi talk on FOXLA News about an idea I had. Is this real???

Stranger things have happened.

👜 👜 👜

Carlos Mencia (@carlosmencia)
Was born in Honduras immigrated to America, and now here I am front row of the @Lakers Game! How fortunate am I

The only problem I've really ever had with immigrants is that some-times they come over here and tell jokes that sound suspiciously simi-lar to our jokes, and don't admit it, even when pressed on the issue on Marc Maron's podcast. In case I wasn't being specific enough, I am talking solely about Carlos Mencia.

🐌 🐌 🐌

Tara Dublin (@taradublinrocks)
Today basically started w an email from Patton Oswalt & ends-ish with a FB friend request from a member of Modest Mouse. #HowIsThisMyLife

You presumably have a job where you book bands and comedians, or work for someone who does?

🐌 🐌 🐌

Hayley Williams (@yelyahwilliams)
What ME?! On the cover of Cosmo? noooo…YESSSSSS! It's true! I'll be on the May issue. Gap teeth and all!

Take this down zero notches. Jk, take it down all of the notches ever.

🐌 🐌 🐌

Grant Imahara (@grantimahara)
Jamie and I are in a limo headed to meet

First Lady Michelle Obama and Dr. Biden.
#thingsineverthoughtidsay

. . . because you thought it may be distasteful to do so?

Case One (@Caseone)
My own room, in a suite, on a 4 star golf course resort in
Palm Springs for a music festival. Oh how things have
changed. #notghettoanymore

Bragging is kiiiinda ghetto actually.

scullin (@scullin)
yup...I'm a keynote speaker at HEC today then i dj at le
scopitone tonight. #whoami?

You. Are. SCULLIN. (Who the fuck is Scullin?)

Greg Garbowsky (@greggarbo)
I'm at the head of a table with jayz beyonce, and bono.
who let me into this party? #namedropping

That is cool that you are genuinely friends with the three of them.

Aaron M. Renn (@urbanophile)
An uncomfortably large number of people seem to be googling my name today. Was it something I said?

You check to see how many people Google you every day?

LeBron James (@KingJames)
Man I'm just a kid from Akron, OH. Wow I'm truly blessed

Yes, you are just a kid from Akron, Ohio, . . . who completely abandoned his home team in an extremely tasteless way on national television. Way to add insult to injury to the people of Ohio! You tha king!

Arlo Hemphill (@arlohemphill)
Today started w/ the governor of Maryland tweeting about me & closed with a big Hollywood PR firm pitching to represent me. Why? No Clue!

You couldn't find out why from the governor's tweet or at the meeting with the PR firm? Open your eyes and ears, brotha!

Ugh, I'm So Humble!

L et's simplify things a bit. Sometimes people just outright call themselves humble. These aren't the typical "brag about something and then insult yourself to soften the blow" type of humblebrags. But, I feel like brags where someone uses the word "humble" should get some sort of automatic inclusion. So here are a few of those...

Amar'e Stoudemire (@Amareisreal)
The NY economy is up 15%. The Knicks are now the most Valuable team N the NBA up 12%. I'm very great full 2 help the NYK & State.

In this case, Amar'e replaced the word "humble" with "grateful" and then replaced the word "grateful" with the words "great full." Regardless of word choice, his main point is that he singlehandedly increased a state's revenue by 15 percent. I don't know if that's true or not (my money's on not), but it's not a very modest thing to say.

FLYONEL RITCHIE (@CDOUGLASROBERTS)
Whatever city I'm in, I just ride thru the hood sometimes.
Like dig them kids use to be me.
Humbling…

You sound like a terrible travel companion.

Jordan Carlos (@jordancarlos)
Wow! Just asked to speak on panel about making a
living in comedy w/ Tim Blake Nelson & John Krasinski.
Wha?????! Humbling :)

Humbling for them too probs.

Reeve Carney (@reevecarney)
I may have sung in front of 30 million people on Idol
tonight, but now I'm in the middle seat on the red-eye
back to NYC. #Stayinghumble

*Status report since this update: Reeve Carney is still having to stay
humble.*

Janelle Monae (@JanelleMonae)
Humbled.

'Nuff said!

* * *

Lil' Dre (@SouljaBoy)
so many new fans. WOW. humbled, thankful & blessed...
Iove you all....June 14!

We are equally as surprised as you appear to be, Soldier.

* * *

vinny milano (@baldvinny)
wow, just realized that the two "bold names" on the
#HighSocks fundraiser event page are @nickswisher and
me! #Humbling #IAmNotWorthy

Who cares, though?

* * *

Eric Cantor (@EricCantor)
Humbled by the trust of my colleagues to serve as
Majority Leader; I am eager to get to work and start
delivering results!

You didn't.

I only quote myself (@XavierSilas)
Im humble because I've been through darkness that most
wouldn't be able to handle. I've felt things that hearts
shouldn't feel. That's why.

Bragging about having gone through "darkness." Interesting take,
weirdo.

Ugh, It's So Weird Getting Recognized!

According to the following famous people, it is QUITE the annoyance to get recognized in public. My heart goes out to them. And according to the following people I've never heard of, it is just as annoying for them to get recognized in public. My heart goes out to them as well. And according to Jim, marriage can be tricky. (Is this show still on? Is this too old a reference?)

Pete Wentz (@petewentz)
Pumping gas in front of the papparazzi makes me way nervous.

You'd think having a bunch of dick pics of you leaked on the Internet would take the edge off a simple gas pump sighting.

Dane Cook (@danecook)
Being famous and having a fender bender is weird. You want to be upset but the other drivers just thrilled & giddy that it's you.

So that narrows down the person you got into an accident with to an eighteen-year-old sorority girl or a nineteen-year-old sorority girl.

Matt Braunger (@Braunger)
"Aren't you that comedian? What are you doing in a Barnes & Noble?" #TooBaffledToAnswer

Acceptable answers: "Hello," "Yes," or "Looking for a book."

Adam Levine (@adamlevine)
Wow. We got mobbed at the airport. I think they thought we were @justinbieber...

They probably thought you were that band that is basically as popular as Justin Bieber.

Amy Dumas (@AmyDumas)
Just got rockognized by a Goodwill employee while making a donation. That stuff is already in his car.....

Nice play on the word "recognized" I think? Wait, are you in a rock band? Who are you? What just happened?

Tinie Tempah (@TinieTempah)
I can't do the 'mean stare' @ bad drivers in traffic
anymore cos they jus go 'Oh look its Tinie Tempah' &
start waving, then I wave bk. :-(

At first I was all "Who the fuck is Tinie Tempah?" Then I looked him up and saw that he is a British rapper. Still, I can't help but feel like I wouldn't know who he was even if I were British.

Noel Clarke (@NoelCarke)
That awkward moment when the pizza man, starts
saying he knows you. "you don't know me, just gimme my
food" LOL

Another British fellow I don't know. His name is Noel Clarke and he's an actor. I've pretty much only seen the British Office *and then roughly the first ninety seconds of* Downton Abbey, *so I'm admittedly not up on my Brit culture. However, even if this guy were wildly famous, this is still a pretty egregious humblebrag.*

Sophie Turner (@sophieRRturner)
Just got recognised in London...weird...

A British trifecta! Judging from her spelling of the word "recognized," I surmised that she is actually from the UK, so getting "recognized" there isn't actually all that weird.

Jason Whitlock (@WhitlockJason)
Just had another "who is this guy" moment. Justin Bieber's bodyguard stopped to speak to me. Justin: "Who is that guy?"

What was the first "who is this guy" moment? JK, don't give a shit.

Jennifer Field (@JenniferField)
Wow feelin loved. Kinda like it! :|~ got recognized three times today! But dont let narcisissm get best of me...or else!

Okay...we won't let narcissism...get the best...of you?

Bit Funk (@BitFunk)
It always feels a little odd to me when I get recognized randomly in public. I never know what to say. I'm glad it doesn't happen often.

Aw, man. I was gonna say "luckily it doesn't happen often," but then you said it. Taking all my lines, dude!

Jane Randall (@JaneRandall15)
Recognized a gagillion times today...even two casting directors said they were fans #thisneverhappens

Well, there's a last time for everything!

Chris Colfer (@chriscolfer)
There is not a word strong enough to describe being
randomly searched at the airport with 25 paparazzi
dudes behind you...

There's a word for humblebragging about it.

Nolan Gould (@Nolan_Gould)
I just had my first screaming girl encounter. She probably
had me confused with someone else.

This is the kid from Modern Family. *It's kind of shitty putting a*
child in here probably, but he's gotta learn sometime.

Kerry Rhodes (@kerryrhodes)
Just got embarrussed on flight! Flight attendant made an
announcement about me being inducted and everybody
got up and applauded. #teamshy!

If it makes you feel any better, I don't know who you are offhand,
and I refuse to Google it.

Nolan D. Smith (@NdotSmitty)
It's crazy how a waiter or waitress service can change,
once they find out who you are! Smh! Treat me the same
please!

*This tweet is somewhere in between war and famine, in terms of
level of awfulness.*

Craig Brenner (@craig_a_brenner)
At a wedding & met someone who says he is a "fan" of
mine. Crazy part is he isn't even related to me. I know I
crapped my pants too

Yes, I crapped my pants from lack of caring about this.

Ugh, I Hate People Wanting My Picture and Autograph All the Time!

I don't pretend to know just how annoying it is to be hounded in public. But I do know that if my job was to be seen and liked by as many people as possible, I wouldn't complain about a bunch of people seeing and liking me. Comes with the territory, famous people.

Sympathy WITHHELD!

Lindsay Lohan (@lindsaylohan)
Omg, I'm so embarrassed, paparazzi just blinded me with flashes again, as I was walking into dinner. They pushed me and I tripped :(hurt…

Going with the ol' "falling over cause of the camera flashes" story, eh?

Wes Rucker (@wesrucker247)
Reason No. 793 SEC fans are college sports' craziest: Tonight was the 4th time in 2 months a fan asked ME to be in a picture with them.

Too much math. Don't feel like wrapping my head around it, but I know it's a humblebrag.

🐑 🐑 🐑

Joe Jonas (@joejonas)
Totally walked down the wrong escalator at the airport from the flashes of the cameras...Go me

Suuuure. Blame it on the flashes.

🐑 🐑 🐑

Rich Eisen (@richeisen)
I've arrived at Letterman and was greeted by a wall of paparazzi, all of them no doubt disappointed I'm not Kate Hudson

This one was just true.

🐑 🐑 🐑

Rihanna (@rihanna)
Excited Fans and papz beating on the car! I couldn't even get out to do an interview on LIVE radio!

I am going to abstain from making a Chris Brown joke here. In fact I am going to abstain from addressing this humblebrag entirely. Instead, I am going to take this time to say to you, Rihanna, if you are read-

ing this: You are beautiful and talented and wonderful and there is no need to go back to Chris. I don't care how good he dances. You don't need him. You can come stand under my umbrella. (NOTE: At the time that this book was written, Rihanna had gotten back together with Chris Brown and the world was very upset about it.)

Rio Ferdinand (@rioferdy5)
Open training session tomorrow....just getting my left hand ready for a colossal signing session afterwards at the stadium! #handache

Man, I really hope this didn't pan out for him.

Van Hatchell (@vandhatch)
Still not used to this question: "Can I have your autograph?"

Not being a dick, but in the long run, might be smart for you to stay not used to it?

Timothy Edington (@the_timbo_slice)
Got asked for my autograph at lunch at Popeye's. I don't think I'll ever get used to that.

Signing your receipt or what?

The Miz (@mikethemiz)
I love when I get stopped for 10 minutes to take a picture because the person doesn't know how to use their own camera.

Hey man, we had to stop and watch you for the fifteen minutes you were famous. You can give us ten.

Drizzy Drake (@drakkardnoir)
Sorry if you've ever worked up all your courage to ask for a picture and I wasn't able to take it right then. I hate being that guy.

I love his assumption that people are always stressfully mustering up courage to ask for a picture every time someone asks him for one. Some people just see the guy from that Sprite commercial and think a photo would be kind of cool.

Kerry Butler (@KerryButlerNyc)
I've been signing so many autographs lately, that I was

writing a card to my dad and started to write my last name!!

But he already KNOWS your last name!!! LOLOL

Jason Mercier (@JasonMercier)
Guy asks for an autograph on break, I oblige and proceed to get marker on my hand...#whenwillitend

The brag was on point. The humble needs some work, though. Marker on the hand? Pretty weak complaint, dude.

Jesse Tyler Ferguson (@jessetyler)
To the fans who wanted to take a picture of me in the Sistine Chapel today: I am honored but "LOOK UP. THERE IS SOMETHING WAY MORE AMAZING!"

This is pretty tacky, man.

Chester M. Hanks (@CHETHAZE)
Holy shit i just got snapped by a paparazzi! First time that has ever happened not in the presence of pops

This is rapper Chet Haze, aka Tom Hanks's son. This tweet pretty much just exposes all his deeply rooted issues and I feel kind of bad for including him in this book. But, also, whatever.

Donald J. Trump (@realDonaldTrump)
People ask me every day to pose for pictures but the camera never works the first time--they are never prepared or maybe just very nervous!

You're an idiot. (Not clever, but he is one!)

Ugh, Several Things!
(The Multi-Humblebrag)

There is a rare type of humblebrag that doesn't fit into any one category and that is the "multi-humblebrag." It is when the offender manages to humblebrag in multiple ways in one tweet. It is truly an art. Amateur humblebraggers need not bother. This is for the pros. I don't know how some of these folks managed to pack in such a high density of humblebragging into 140 characters, but bravo, ladies and sirs. Here are several examples. I will do my best to guide you through them and show you why they qualify.

David Nail (@davidnail)
I'm staring at a Popeyes right now! This is taking such will power! David, expensive suit, red carpet, tv, skinnyness! K, I can do it!

Red carpet, TV, expensive suit, being skinny—this one is a real minefield. Everywhere you step there's a humblebrag.

John Papa (@John_Papa)
one thing that sucks about getting fit is that my clothes
dont fit and they are expensive :(

That's two things, homeboy (that you're in shape and that you have money, just to clarify). You also gotta love the kicker at the end: the frowny face.

Sean Agnew (@TheRealFagnew)
Yooooooo holy shit! I am at the craziest house party at
coachella with jose canseco and beyonce. So weird.

This is an evolution of the classic "weird" humblebrag because he's also dropping names. Also, I'm sure both Jose and Beyoncé enjoyed your lingering stares.

Mightypeter (@Mightypeter)
Did anyone see the E! broadcast of the Creative Arts
Emmys? Did I look like an idiot?

This is a brag about how he is on television (though it's the E! network, so…meh), that he is at an awards show (though it's not even the actual Emmys), and lastly he is "genuinely" asking whether or not he looked like an idiot, basically compliment fishing to all of America. Pretty good job, Mightypeter!

Sharon Hinnendael (@SharonHinnendae)
Sooo ackward being hit on while in line to pick up my
birth control while holding #tampons and #Midol...
Whyyyyy????

This is a multi-humblebrag about being hit on; it uses the word
"ackward" (I think she means awkward); and as a bonus, men-
tioning birth control implies she has a lot of sex.

Amy Berg (@bergopolis)
Just came up with a series idea that is either totally
insane or totally awesome. Can't possibly do three pilots
this year, can I?

This one is about how smart she is ("totally awesome") and also
how successful her TV career is going (THREE pilots???!?). Any-
ways, as it turned out, she could not, in fact, do three pilots.

J. J. Watt (@JJWatt)
Tim McGraw concert now with @BlaineGabbert after
dinner with the President. Crazy, just a kid from small-
town Wisconsin. #HardWorkPaysOff

I don't blame him for his excitement. That's a ton of cool shit in a
twenty-four-hour period. If I correctly remember the day he tweeted
this, all I did was eat four tacos, thought about doing laundry,

and added some stuff to my Netflix queue. (And I'm even lying about the laundry and the Netflix.)

Jay Light (@DietJay)
Thankfully, it was a lot less awkward the second time I talked to John C. Reilly. For my (mental) health. #Cannes

This is about how Jay Light is at the exclusive Cannes Film Festival and a name-drop about talking to John C. Reilly twice. They sound like they are good friends!

Kate Upton (@KateUpton)
Excited for @tacobell all-star celeb softballgame Who would have known I'm model turned pro athlete? I'm thinking I shuld step up my gym time

Model-brag, celeb-brag, exclusive event-brag. The works.

Irina Voronina (@IrinaVoronina)
I think I was on Extra tonight for @vodaswim, but missed it because I was flying to Lima!

Irina managed to brag about three different things in one here. She was on TV, she was endorsing something called "voda swim" (which

I'm guessing is brag-worthy to whoever knows what voda swim is), and she is traveling to Lima. Count 'em. Three things.

🐷 🐷 🐷

Keli Goff (@keligoff)
Despite being pretty used 2 tv I still get all kinds of NERVOUS at book readings. Is that weird?

Top-notch stuff here. A brag about being used to being on TV (implying she is frequently on it) and also that she has a book out. All tied up with the nice tight bow of asking if her nervousness is "weird."

🐷 🐷 🐷

Mark Hayes (@allsop8184)
I wonder how much Goodwill is going to sell my $300 Burberry sweater for?

He's not only letting us now he is charitable person, but that he is a rich charitable person. I feel like this tweet alone cancels out all of his charity work (and by charity work, I mean dropping a sweater in a large box). I am impressed at how much humblebrag he managed to cram into 140 characters.

Ugh, I Travel Too Much!

All right, now let's get back to basics, enough of that multilayered *Inception*-style humblebrag shit. Much like tweeting about flying in first class, what's the point of traveling if you can't brag to someone about it? P.S. No one likes hearing about other people's vacations. You know that feeling you have when someone is like, "Hey, do you want to see pictures of my trip to Cabo?" and you think "No," and then they show you and it's just pictures of beaches and white people dancing at a Señor Frog's? Well, that is also the feeling people get when you tweet about your travel. *If I wasn't there, I don't care.* That's a good mantra to try and remember if you are ever thinking about bragging about cool places you visited to someone who wasn't there.

stacey bendet (@staceybendet)
Sleepless in hong kong!

Unimpressed in LA.

🐷 🐷 🐷

Mark Hanis (@MarkHanis)
Mauritius ✈ Paris ✈ NYC ✈ DC. Oy vay.

This might be the first Yiddish humblebrag. Mazel tov!

John Sloss (@johnsloss)
I'm constantly amazed by the sheer number of fire doors
in London hotels. But then, as you know by now, I'm
easily amazed.

Sounds like you go to London a lot! That was your point, right?

Ted Hope (@TedHope)
Just enough time from teaching in Havana to change
clothes & head to cpenhagen to consult on t future of film.
Whew!

*Teaching?? Havana?? Copenhagen?!? Consulting?!?!? THE
FUTURE OF FILM??!? If I didn't know any better, I'd say you
were bragging.*

Ryan Block (@ryan)
Moving day and I'm sick as hell with some bug I caught
on the way back from France. Glad we hired movers.

*Masterfully done. You snuck that France thing in there with the
finesse of James Bond rolling under a closing door in the nick of time.*

Bernie Su (@BernieSu)
Packing for Hawaii for the weekend...I may be the least excited person going to Hawaii ever.

Subtext: I am a person going to Hawaii.

Tony Rock (@TONYROCK)
My sleep schedule is discombobulated. I wake up in the middle of the night and I'm sleepy in the day. Too much flying all over the globe.

Flying around the world seeing your brother do stand-up I presume? (That was maybe too harsh, and I feel bad, but am leaving it in.)

Christine Kirk (@LuxuryPRGal)
Only slept 5 hours. Town car will be here in 20 minutes. At least I'm headed to Maui instead of traveling somewhere for work...#6AM #Notafan

Can't you just tell us you're going to Maui and be done with it? This was like an SAT math equation. (Granted, the confusion here may be on me a little bit. Simple math is like an SAT equation to me.)

Johnny Weir (@JohnnyGWeir)
It still amazes me that I can be in Prague, London and

the Paramus Whole Foods all in one day. Travel and
technology boggle my mind.

*It boggles your mind that those places are within a day's travel of one
another? Did you send this tweet from the fourteenth century?*

Charles Melton (@_MELTON_)
Will Twitter be available for me in Paris, milan, or the
Maldives? I hope so bc it won't in hong Kong or Singapore

Shut up, dude. Trust me.

Stephen Fry (@stephenfry)
Well I'm at CDG, Paris, hoping to catch the connection to
Amsterdam. Rather a full schedule in NL of readings &
signings & me all unshaven.

*It's people like you that perpetuate the stereotype that people from
the Netherlands don't shave!*

Lindsey N Waterhouse (@Linds777)
My emails send so slowly over here in Cannes! So
frustrated!

Luckily your tweets about how you are at Cannes came through juuuust fine. (I'm guessing that's all your emails said too.)

Jeff Raileanu (@jraileanu)
Gelato shop insisted that I take a frequent customer card
because I'm there so often. I don't spend *that* much time
in Florence, do I?

Gelato frequent customer cards don't lie! (FUN FACT: That was the original title of Shakira's hit song "Hips Don't Lie.")

Repeat Offenders

Some people humblebrag with such a high frequency that I wanted to devote a whole section to them. Some of these repeat offenders only did it a couple of times, but the quality was so high that it was like the equivalent of a thousand garden-variety humblebrags. They're in here too. Enjoy.

Sohaib Athar (@ReallyVirtual)

This is the fellow who was blogging from Pakistan during the Osama Bin Laden raid. He's like the 1,400th most famous kind-of-sort-of audio witness arguably ever, so yeah—pretty big deal.

Fact: I don't own a TV set and stopped watching TV many years ago. Sorry three-lettered-big-tv-news-channels for not replying to your emails

I love people who talk about how they don't own a TV. I think it's cool, new and edgy. Just kidding.

oh I forgot, one needs electricity to make coffee, which, we don't have right now in Abbottabad. :-/

Hey man, you wouldn't happen to be in Abbottabad right now, would you?

and here come the mails from the mainstream media...*sigh*

Sigh.

Uh oh, now I'm the guy who liveblogged the Osama raid without knowing it.

This guy's fifteen minutes cannot end soon enough for me—oh, what's that? They're over? Cool.

Jamie Kilstein (@jamiekilstein)

Jamie Kilstein is a comedian who works hard and is a nice guy. This is not a knock on his comedy. It is a knock on his humblebragging about his comedy. Whatever happened to letting achievements speak for themselves?

Sorry to be namedroppy but if it wasn't for robin williams pep talk tonight I may have quit comedy. Weird night.

One of my favorite humblebrags is when the attempted brag isn't even all that cool. Not sure how "namedroppy" Robin Williams is in 2011, but solid try no less!

Taping an mma show and waiting in oprahs bff gayles dressing room. #soweirdidontknowwhattodo

*Just hang in there and try to pretend you are in a place that is only
very minimally noteworthy. Oh, wait.*

Greg graffin from bad religion emailed me after conan.
More importantly this means bad religion watches conan!

*Oh, don't be coy: MOST importantly, Greg Graffin from Bad Reli-
gion emailed you. You can just say it. It's cool, dawg.*

Whenever I have a meeting with someone in the industry
and they pick a fancy place I immediately feel like I'm
going to be kicked out

Which industry, yo?

I was mentioned in the NY times but the piece was so
fucking dumb I didn't post it. All though he said nice
things about me. #burningbridges

*Yeah, but you just mentioned the piece, so clearly you wanted us to know
about it. The only bridge burned here is the one between you and humility.*

Countdown to me pacing in the green room wondering
what the fuck happened and how I got here.

*This one sounds like the opening voice-over from a biopic about a
country singer I wouldn't see.*

Tila Tequila (@OfficialMsTila)

Tila Tequila was the girl who was famous for being bisexual. For anyone who was curious what she was up to after her show about giving/receiving herpes went off the air, here is what she was up to.

I hate my lambo! Police is ALWAYS pulling me over just cuz its a lambo so they always think I'm speeding but I'm not!! Then they let me go!

Stop it.

I think they just wanna talk to me....Ughhhh! Ok I'm done with this lambo! I'm buying a 1988 brown toyota corolla!!!! Lmao! I swear!

Please stop it.

Man this is SO unfair! Why did the lambo dealership not tell me I'd get pulled over at least once a week in this car? Time for a corolla lol!

Seriously, please?

I should be alseep cuz early call time tomorrow but instead I'm still up eating all the damn food I bought earlier from grocery store! Lmao!

Okay, I'm just gonna go.

H. J. Adams (@hjadams1)

No clue who H. J. Adams is. I know he is the most secure man on the planet (he willfully goes by the name "HJ"). But, I also know that he seems like the type who may come find me and kill me (sounds like he has the build of a football player).

His bio does say that he is from "Hogwarts," which at least means he has a sense of humor. (Or is a wizard. If he is in fact a wizard, hopefully he's from Gryffindor and not Slytherin—those guys are ruthless. Damn, shit got nerdy up in here!)

> Every single time i go to the gym someone asks me what position i play. I dont play football, stop asking!

I know he says he is annoyed when people ask him if he plays football, but I am going to go out on a limb and say that this guy probably—hear me out—actually maybe, may in fact, like people thinking that he plays football.

> Just got asked to hangout w/dwight howard and a bunch of other nba players tonite. Never done this before. What do i wear? Help!

Basketball attire! JK! Who cares!

Donald Glover (@DonaldGlover)

Donald Glover is a writer turned actor turned rapper. One of the first humblebraggers on the Twitter feed. A true pioneer of the humblebrag game!

> Fart #thingsItriednottodoinfrontofAnnaWintour
> They sat me next to Anna Wintour for the
> @bandofoutsiders fashion show…
> Texting dad about sitting next to Anna Wintour
> #thingsItriednottodoinfrontofAnnaWintour

Does anyone know if Donald Glover was seated next to Anna Wintour at this fashion show?

Okay, these next two tweets are extra special because they are the aforementioned first ever retweets on the Humblebrag Twitter feed. Where it all began…

> Its an honor to be the 1st thing japanese men see
> after reading their porn on the subway RT @Pishogue:
> #biginjapan
> Getting to see my GAP Christmas ad. It was the
> 2nd hottest day in NYC when we shot it. I hope they
> photoshopped out the crotch sweat…

Donald later referenced "humblebrag" in one of his songs, so now all of this is just one big giant feedback loop.

Joshua Horowitz (@joshuahorowitz)

Joshua Horowitz brags about meeting celebrities like it's his job...which it actually is I guess. He's an MTV reporter or something, but still...

> I just confused Angelina Jolie so many times in the course of my interview I'm pretty sure she has a migraine.

Two cookies!
(Lemme explain: Whenever I read Josh Horowitz's tweets, I feel a weird impulse to yell out how many cookies he should be rewarded.)

> I get it. You're the coolest man on the planet!! Enough!— what I resisted saying when I met Johnny Depp (smoking, gold teeth) today.

Seven cookies!

> Back to work tomorrow means Mila Kunis is stopping by. #notcomplaining Questions?

Four cookies!

> Harvey Weinstein is sitting at the next table. Mila Kunis waved to me from a nearby table. Something is WRONG in the universe. #gothamawards

One thousand cookies!

Lee Unkrich (@leeunkrich)

Lee Unkrich is the insanely talented Pixar director (*Toy Story 3*, *Finding Nemo*). He is also an insanely talented humble-braggart.

> Spaz Alert: I tripped walking up stairs to stage to receive my Oscar Nominee certificate. #foreveranerd

Supposing he means "forever a nerd" and not "for Eve Ranerd," this hashtag really solidifies this as a humblebrag. I'm guessing the tweet isn't for Eve Ranerd. She doesn't exist.

> Did this actually happen? I have absolutely no recollection of Justin Timberlake bowing down to me.

He then attached a picture of Timberlake bowing to him onstage at the Oscars as he receives his statue. And to answer your question, Lee, yes, the guy from The Love Guru *bowed down to you.*

> Just in case you think all this has gone to my head, within 36 hours of winning the Oscar, I was back home plunging a clogged toilet.

Does anyone know if Lee Unkrich won an Oscar? Please email me at jk@obviously.com.

> I'm so hungry, I'm going to eat my BAFTA. #StuckInCarOnWayToParty

Bonus BAFTA brag!

Jake Owen

Jake Owen is a country singer I think. I've never heard of him, but apparently some woman at a diner has...

> just crushed an omelet.... even after some lady leaned over my table asking for an autograph and dipped her boob in my hashbrowns. Yum.

What part of this do you think he was more excited to tell us? That he ate an omelet or that some woman asked him for an autograph? I bet it's the autograph thing.

Jake Owen also frequently employs "some person did something great and I am very good friends with them" type of humblebrag.

> Hey y'all.. Tryin to get a trend started for my best bud Mardy Fish playing his 3rd match at US Open.. Come on y'all! cheer him on! #gofishy
> Congrats to @Miranda_Lambert for all 9 of her CMA nominations. I don't know anyone more deserving.
> Watching @blakeshelton perform on late night TV right now...He's a damn fine singer and a great guy. Congrats on the success buddy.

You know country singers and a tennis player??? Right on, dude.

Kurt Warner (@kurt13warner)

Former NFL quarterback, Kurt Warner, continues his streak of being really annoying...

> Grocery store I shop at still sells my t-shirt so I am getting chased from aisle 2 aisle 4 autograph! Ppl I retired, send them back!
> Sitting in locker room w/ Jerry rice, Herschel Walker, John Randle, @marshallfaulk, etc...I must still b fooling ppl that I belong here!
> Here in CR @ZachJohnsonPGA charity event...
> Thousands came out 2 watch me golf, huh? Scared I am going 2 hurt someone...FOUR!!!!!!!!!!!!!!!!

I guess he should be commended on being able to say three statements without thanking Jesus.

LeVar Burton (@levarburton)

Just a quick intro...these next two are two of my all-time favorites. They aren't your standard definition of a "humblebrag." They are sort of mislead-brags, but they were too good to not include. If you are truly upset that they were included despite not being conventional humblebrags, then you are a weirdo.

It's a good night for natural light in LA...

Look at this beauty. Just for a second remember how pointless it is to post a picture of a fireplace, and then look at all those awards. Also, he is indoors. Why is this a particularly "good" night? Love this one.

The stockings still hung...

We get it—you got some Emmys for Reading Rainbow. *Relax, man.*

Oprah Winfrey (@Oprah)

Oprah Winfrey is the most famous anything in the history of anything. She is a walking achievement. There is no need for her to humblebrag, and yet...

> I most want to thank @DrMayaAngelou for helping me be brave. In my most fearful moments she has been the one I relied on most & called 1st.

Point taken, Oprah. Maya Angelou is your butt buddy. Chill out.

> Toronto, THANK YOU, I leave with a grateful heart.
> And joyful Spirit. I felt blessed by your presence. 17,000 blessings In one day!

Okayyyy, point taken once again, Oprah: you're a DRAW. Sheesh.

> OMG! Just had a SURPRISE date with Jackie Jackson. My teen idol hearthrob. Tried not to talk too much or eat too much. Succeeded at neither!

Oprah, you don't gotta brag, boo. You're Oprah.

Jeff Donovan (@Jeffrey_Donovan)

I wasn't sure who Jeff Donovan was, and then I looked him up and realized why I don't know who he is. He is on *Burn Notice*, and I have never seen *Burn Notice*. I'm guessing he is also a writer on *Burn Notice*. He tells amazing stories. Check out this thrill ride:

> So worked out w trainer..leaving (paparazzi looking for Tom Cruise) tries to get a photo of me (hate) I run to car and he says!:(2bcont)?
>
> I jump in car and he is upset I don't want photo. He says 'what the fuck u r not even that famous!' God forgive these lost souls...
>
> CLARIFICATION: NO!! he didn't think I WAS Tom Cruise!! He was bored looking for him. Thought he could shoot me.
>
> 'IRONY' : when a paparazzi yells at celeb.. 'don't hide you're not that famous' in order to get a photo.

What an odyssey of humility!

Julia Allison

I don't have a complete handle on who Julia Allison is. I know she lives in New York and that she seems to know a lot of people and that she writes things sometimes. Humblebrags, specifically.

> Just watched the Oxygen pilot I shot last Feb. Ugh. Verdict is in: I have a face for radio. Finally, something my haters & I can agree on!

Face for the radio? But you were in a TV pilot. You just told us that.

The "green room" I'm sitting in at CBS bears an uncanny resemblance to a prison.

Find the biggest guy, stab him in the neck with a pen, and earn the other inmates' respect. You'll be fine.

ARGHHGHGHGH! And now I have a big audition out in LA. So next week is: Chicago, New York, LA. United Elite Status WILL BE MINE.

Hey! I thought you said you had a face for the radio! What are you doing at an audition?

No. More. TRAVEL!!!!!!!!! no nooooo noooooo!

Julia speaks about traveling to cool cities with the same terror one would about being sexually assaulted and/or witnessing a loved one die.

J. Michael Straczynski (@straczynski)

J. Michael Straczynski wrote *Thor.* And then these:

Finished one big project was going to take a breather before the next one, got whomped with new idea in the shower I now have to write. WTF?

Arghgh, prisoner of your own genius! Arghghgh.

The interview was plagued with technical difficulties: no
matter what they did to the camera, you could still see
me on-screen. Tragic.

*Writers don't get to be on-screen that often, and when they do, they
say stuff like that.*

Going to Lake Arrowhead tomorrow to speak at Writers
Guild conference, my topic: surviving as a writer. Dunno
if I'll survive the experience

Why won't you survive?

Tyler, The Creator (@fucktyler)

Odd Future (aka OFWGKTA) is a relatively new rap group
who got famous for bein' so *ka-raaaazzzzyyyy*! Anyway,
front man Tyler, The Creator is so *ba-raaaaggggyyyy*!

Hahaha, Frank And I Are Nominated For A BET Award.....
Weird...

Is it? Is it really?

My Moonman Still Husnt Come In The Mail. =(

*By "Moonman," he is referring to the statuette you get when you
win an MTV award. Then he adds a frowny face emoticon. Very
relatable.*

It's All Happening So Fast. I'm Only 19. Fuck, When I Hit
24 Or Something What Am I Gonna Look Forward Too?
Shit. #newgoals

Them's the breaks, kid!

I've Tried Everything To Get Out Of This Rolling Stone
Shoot Tomorrow. Maybe I'll Get Arrested On Purpose.
Yeah, Swag.

Or just do the shoot because you really want to.

Fuck Like 50k People Paid Money To Listen To Me Bitch
About Life And Talk About Immature Shit Over Repetitive
Beats.... This Is Fucking Crazy

Are you talking about your music or something else?

Nothing More Corny That Being In A Magazine And The
Whole Concept Is 'The New Face Of Hip Hop' With Some
Other Rappers You Dont Really Like

Rough, dude.

I HOPE THEY DONT THINK IM A DICK, ITS JUST LIKE
MAN NOW I GOTTA SIT ON THE BUS BORED CAUSE IF I
GO OUT ILL GET BUMRUSHED FOR PHOTOS AND SHIT

*For someone that hates recognition you sure did release an album,
tour, and tweet an awful lot.*

Kid Just Told Me I Was His Hero. That Shit Is Awkward As Fuck, I'm Just A Regular Nigga. Damn Thats Weird.

I can't really say too much about this one due to his word choice, but it's a humblebrag.

I Hope They Don't Ask For A Photo. I Just Wanna Buy This Movie A Go On With My Day, Cause Then 50 More People Will Ak For One. Fuck

I assure you that fifty-one people in any given video store do not know who OFWGTA is.

How Do I Say 'No I Don't Want To Take A Photo, I Am Eating With My Friends, Leave Me The Fuck Alone Dude' To A Supporter Of Me, In Public?

Say it to the person asking for a photo, not to Twitter.

So I Have To Fly Out This Week, I Didn't Know What Fashion Week Was Until About 3 Hours Ago. Not My Kinda Party, Gonna Be Awkward

Look, I can't give him too much shit. He was born in 1991. He is twenty years old. If I got famous when I was twenty, I'd also be all "I'm famous!" But still, it's like, we get it, man—you're popular! At ease, soldier!

Meghan McCain (@McCainBlogette)

Meghan McCain is John McCain's daughter. She disagrees with her dad on a lot of issues, so she isn't completely terrible. But she does humblebrag an awful lot.

Thank you so much to everyone that came out @ the Miami book fair. So awesome to meet all my amazing readers. Now I have 2 go ice my hand...

Or try having less fans! JK, that's impossible. Your book is great!

I understand that I look about 19 without makeup on, but seriously lady I can't look THAT much different on @maddow than in person.

On behalf of this "lady," I'm sorry, but your youthful appearance is not only confounding, but downright infuriating!

wanna know what's awkward? when jeremy piven starts dating some chick that apparently looks like me and my phone starts going off. #stupid

Guhhhh tell me about it.

"she's that republican, the one with the rack" #icanhearyouasshole #thisismylife

Sorry 'bout them tits!

> never know what I'm gonna get when people approach
> me - I'm either the patron saint of new republicanism or
> the party's young antichrist ;-)

*Let's take it easy with the referring to yourself as a "saint" of any
kind.*

*All that aside, if you are a blond Republican girl, I'm probably
going to have a shameful attraction to you.*

Tyrese Gibson (@Tyrese)

Tyrese is a model, actor, singer, baker, cobbler, coppersmith...
you name it he is it.

> If my tweets are a roadmap to a better YOU.. I accept this
> with pride.. All I can do is try my best.. 140 characters at
> a time..

*I never said anything about your tweets being a road map to a better
anything. You did, man. If anything, your tweets are my road map
to a worse day.*

> Money doesn't make you happy.. Having AMAZING
> PEOPLE in your LIFE while you have money makes you
> happy..

*Now, admittedly I am no detective, but it seems like you are imply-
ing that you have lots of money.*

David Wild (@Wildaboutmusic)

David Wild is some sort of music journalist or something of the sort. If you've ever seen the Metallica documentary *Some Kind of Monster* (if you haven't you really should), the band hires a therapist who essentially winds up thinking that he is the fifth member of the band. His delusions are heartbreaking. Anyway, that is kind of the vibe I get from David Wild.

> I just had my picture taken with Snooki. Because Joan Didion isn't backstage.

The first ever Snooki-brag?? Also, fifty points for casually throwing in a "backstage" there at the end.

> Got home, turned on TV & saw myself on "Motley Crue: Behind The Music." I'm the one who didn't do drugs or groupies, yet aged the worst.

Also the one who wasn't in the band, and whom no one knows or cares about.

> My wife's agreed to attend the Oscars with me 4 the 1st time. You can't miss us. She will be the pretty lady. I'll be the schmuck in a tux.

What I like about this one is the not-so-subtle way in which David Wild lets us know he has been to many Oscars. This humblebrag has a nice calling-yourself-a-schmuck finish. Great stuff all around.

Dana Brunetti (@DanaBrunetti)

Dana Brunetti is a producer in Hollywood who is a down-right gold mine for this stuff. Luckily, he tweeted once about being called out for humblebragging and seems to have a sense of humor about it. So here ya go.

> Enroute DGA awards via @a_McCallie. My car was sent to wrong address on other side of town :-/

Judging from the forward slash frowny face, one can surmise that he is none too pleased about his personal car service being on the wrong side of town when it is supposed to be taking him to the Directors Guild Awards

> Wow! I just won a Golden Globe!

On the surface this may just seem like a regular brag, but if you inspect closely you'll see that the "wow" implies a humble sense of shock or surprise, as if to say "Whaaaat? Meeeee?"

> My Gold Level Starbucks card arrived the same day as my Golden Globe. Coincidence? I don't think so.

Does this mean you drink so much coffee that it allowed you to work hard enough to win a Golden Globe? Just checking.

> Wow. I'm in Sundance and nominated for an Oscar. Bet I will still have trouble getting into the after parties here.

Got some nice double-humblebrag action with the Sundance and the Oscar nomination of it all. For those wondering, Dana got into the parties just fine.

Jesse Peyronel (@JesseDir)

Jesse Peyronel is a director who is so busy directing that he doesn't even have time to finish the word "director" in his Twitter name!

> Yes, this is me and #thesituation at the GQ man of the year party

(Attached here was a picture of Jesse and The Situation at said party.)

   The "yes" here implies a sort of "can you believe it?" sentiment. So, yes, I can believe that The Situation let you take a picture with him.

> At the GQ Man Of The Year party at chateau.
> I am the only non-famous person here.
> Casts of glee, social network, @Sethmacfarlane, @oliviamunn, J Knoxville…Everyone was at the #GQmanoftheyear party last night. And me.

Dude, chill out about the GQ party. I lost count of the number of shits people don't give.

Justin Bieber (@justinbieber)

I can't really fault Biebs for bragging. He is eleven. That is what they do, but nevertheless...

> im from a small town many have never heard of...my
> parents had me as teenagers...me and my my mom lived
> in a small apartment...
> no one in my family had really left my town or the area
> and i never thought leaving was possible....but then u
> all found me....
> and you all changed my life and showed me opportunity
> i didnt think existed. you taught me to #dreambig and
> #neversaynever. so thank u

There is a chance he is being genuine here. There is also a chance his PR person wrote this for him. Either way, dude needs to take it down a notch.

> thinking about having a movie night...everyone wants to
> watch #NeverSayNever3D.....im mean im down...but is
> that weird? lol.

I promise you no one wants to watch that and are just trying to please their boy king. Veto the movie, they'll thank you.

Olivia Munn (@oliviamunn)

Olivia Munn is a model/*Daily Show* correspondent? I dunno, man, but it's true.

#2 on @MaximMag Hot 100? Holy moly. Thanks!!! Does
this mean I have 2 stop eating pie now?...Because I
won't.

Ah, the ol' thin-girl-saying-she-loves-pie routine.

Finished Saturday shopping, but some cameras outside
& Im solo so dont know what 2 do. Sooo went back in 2
keep shopping. Yay more clothes!

*You'd think someone who hates cameras so much wouldn't have
chosen the one profession where your job is to be in front of cameras.*

At GQ Party having fun til 1 douchey girl tries to set up a
guerilla-style photo op w/me.. Bitch, go read a book...or
something smart.

Enjoy this time, Munn.

Eric Stonestreet (@ericstonestreet)
This fellow is one half of the gay couple on *Modern Family*.

Just stood in the oval office. Grateful I didn't fall over a
couch or spill strawberry juice on the rug.

Strawberry juice? Who drinks strawberry juice?

This time a year Im so grateful I dont have 2 worry about
all the pilots I wouldnt have gotten auditions 4. Much
respect n luv fellow actors

You mean, like, because you are on the hit TV show called Modern
Family? *Is that what you mean? Just wanna be clear on what you
meant.*

> I think what would surprise most people at award show
> parties is the sheer amount of farting I'm doing while
> talking to famous people.

*Dude, YOU'RE famous. You crossed over. You aren't an everyman
anymore. Get over it.*

Fiona Fong (@fionafong)
Fiona Fong went to Harvard, I think. Not sure though.

> Can you believe that its already been 3 years since I
> donned my gown and cap and received my Harvard
> diploma??? #harvardclassof2008 #imsoold

*I'm not sure how many people other than you were keeping track,
friend.*

> Is it embarrassing that I'm dying to see the World's
> Largest Dinosaurs exhibit at the Natural History
> Museum? I miss dinos class at Harvard!

*Two in a row. Way to to dispel that stereotype about Harvard alums
bragging about having gone to Harvard . . .*

Rick Warren (@RickWarren)

Rick Warren is a big time evangelical minister.

> Big surprise: 2 Guinness Book of World Records judges came to my office & said I've set a world record in books!

What records? Least books bought by gay people? (I'd imagine Rick Warren probably hates gay people.)

> I'm truly humbled you follow my tweets.I pray they enrich your life &strengthen your ministry.God bless all 200,000 of you!

Jesus has way more followers. Step up your game, homie!

> You know you're CALLED BY GOD to do something when you enjoy even the dull & mundane parts.

Or you're just a weirdo.

will.i.am (@iamwill)

will.i.am is in the group of people called the The Black Eyed Peas.

> Hey dr. Is something wrong with me? Why am I working out at 8am after carnival with no sleep?

This should be like number seventeen on your list of concerns regarding things you're doing wrong in your life.

Christmas shopping today...I haven't been home in 3weeks & now its santa.i.am time...Im blessed to give better presents then I receive...

You hear that, people in will.i.am's life? He thinks you give shitty gifts! Merry xmas!

Arthur Kade (@ArthurKade)

I tried to find out who this guy is by looking at his Wikipedia page and just became all the more confused. He's some sort of financial adviser-model-interviewer-actor. Who knows? He was raised by his grandmother. I know that much at least.

Skipping golden globe after party. Prepping 4 meetings 2mrw about show and want to look and be fresh. Maybe a networking mistake but oh well

Literally every word you chose to use here is the vernacular of a terrible person.

Did I just get a guitar lesson from Stanley Jordan?! Arguably best jazz guitarist in the world 4 Time Grammy nominee

Feels like you're really the only one who can answer that. Sounds like you might've...

Do I seriously have 9 production companies all interested in my concept?? This is amazing. God is great!!

No, you don't.

Also, while many of you are no doubt literally SHOUTING at the top of your lungs right now, "This seems more like a regular brag than a humblebrag. I didn't buy a book about regular brags, Harris, you piece of dumb shit!" The part that qualifies this as a humblebrag is the "seriously." As in, "Seriously, can you believe it? I sure can't believe it! I know, right?!" So, chill out.

Miscellaneous

There are some humblebrags I didn't *quiiite* know what to file under, but they are still worthy of inclusion. This is the section for humblebrags that managed to illicit a negative reaction deep in my gut, but that my brain couldn't process what category they belong in. They are too unique to be confined to a label. These people are truly bragging outside of the box.

Monika Platek (@MonikaPlatek)
My brother's dog just bit my engagement ring. Settle down, pup, it's a diamond not a treat! Still so cute.

You know in a romantic comedy when you want the cool main girl to get the guy, but that guy is engaged to a prissy, blond, ex-sorority president? This tweet reminds me of that blond girl. I'm starting to see a real rise in engagement humblebrags. Not enough to warrant a whole chapter of their own, but be on the look out for them in the future.

dɪplo (@diplo)
So girls are here in my room and im still playing angry
bird i kinda wish they would fall asleep or something

*You know the average American male has a hard time getting just
one girl to even speak to him, right?*

Josh Groban (@joshgroban)
Hey NPR, thanks for saying I have an amazing voice. No
thanks for the snide low blows! #expectedmore

*Learn to take a compliment, Grobes! Didn't quite know where to
file this one, but it needed to be included. Groban humblebragging
an NPR compliment? The stuff dreams are made of (not many
dreams, but a couple maybe).*

Nate Cosby (@NateCosBOOM)
Someone I don't know just randomly emailed to say they
like me & the work I've done. Not sure how to feel. I am
unaccustomed to praise.

Well, this was certainly the wrong instinct to follow.

Kyle Cease (@kylecease)
Going through old stuff n just found my old original script

n call sheet for 10 things I hate about u. Crazy to c me
Heath n Julia together

One Thing I Hate About This Tweet: Everything.

Scott Harrison (@scottharrison)
just got word that we've been invited to ring the opening
bell on the Nasdaq Wednesday Morning (!!!!) must be a
slow day…

*The first NASDAQ humblebrag I've come across. Soooort of
momentous?*

Laney Crowell (@laneycrowell)
Photographed by the one and only Bill Cunningham of
the @nytimes this morning-- with wet hair and no make
up. Really God? Really?

*Blaming God for this? You're like the Jeremy Lin of talking about
your picture being taken. This is Lane-sanity!*

Alexis Ohanian (@kn0thing)
Definitely got refused service at the Yale Club bar bc I'm
wearing jeans. So it goes. Esp amusing given I spoke at
Yale a month ago…

Yale-brag.

Jordan Vogt-Roberts (@VogtRoberts)
Life in LA is an exercise in not being a douchebag part 1: getting a note from an actress that says "I'm yours if the part's mine"

Exercise part 2: Not saying things like this.

Dirk Hayhurst (@TheGarfoose)
Being a player, an artist, or social entity means you get critiqued and judged. I'm all three. Thus, I polarize. At Any rate, thanks-->

Who are you polarizing? When I think "Dirk Hayhurst," I think "baseball player." . . . Because you are a baseball player.

Jaron (@JaronATLRTL)
Every time I'm at the dentists office I hear Celine Dion or Peter Cetera...But this time I hear me!! Ugh.

So stop singing!

Skip Bayless (@RealSkipBayless)
I've never known anyone, in or out of sports, who works out as hard as I do 365 days year after year. I know: I'm nuts. But it's who I am.

Why'd you say this?

David Faustino (@DavidFaustino)
i can always tell how drunk the peeps are on the tour
buses that stop @ my house, by how loud they yell for me
to come out. #BittterSweet

Bud Bundy, y'all! Getting yelled at to come out, y'all!

Almie Rose (@apocalypstick)
Hey James Franco, thanks a lot for looking just like my ex.
Really makes this show better. Hope that fucking boulder
follows you on stage.

*This is interesting because it isn't about she herself being hot, but
about an ex being hot. She's humblebragging for someone else. Addi-
tionally, I'd be curious to hear how many people besides her concur
that her ex looks likes James Franco.*

Josh Gondelman (@joshgondelman)
People always tell my girlfriend that she could be Natalie
Portman's twin. And they tell me I could be her dad.

You look NOTHING like Mr. Portman, sir!

Deepak Chopra (@DeepakChopra)
Hope & despair are born of imagination. I am free of both

I hereby present Deepak Chopra the Award for Innovation in Humble-
bragging. I really love the idea of someone "spiritually" humblebragging.
A real game changer. In case anyone is unclear on this one, the brag is
that he is free of despair and the humble is that he is free from hope.
A masterpiece. Congratulations, Deepak.

Alexandra Comito (@superstarrgurl)
Agh I need an assistant for my social life too! So many
parties coming up...

Just... go to them? Why the stress? Pretty cut and dry.

Katee Sackhoff (@kateesackhoff)
Crap!!! I have to do Voice Over for a new video game
tmrw and I'm getting sick!! My throat is killing me!

Is this the first video game voice-over humblebrag of the book? I
think it is. That's funny.

Chris Schilling (@schillingc)
Disclosure: I do sometimes write for said best games

mag, though it says a lot that they can overcome this handicap to remain so great.

Second video game humblebrag of the book! We're on a nerd roll!

TODOS SOMOS PUTOS (@TODOSSOMOSPUTOS)
Just found out that my artwork was exhibited in an important French museum but 1) it was 1 1/2 yrs ago and 2) I wasn't invited nor told.

Pretty pretentious stuff goin' on here. Or, an attempt at being pretentious. "important French museum" sounds like when a five-year-old is lying.

Mary E. Winstead (@M_E_Winstead)
You often hear actresses say "I lose roles for being too beautiful." I don't ever get that. But I do get "too classy" and "too strong". Hmm.

I don't often hear actresses say that.

miss gigi (@missgigip)
If I get called a motivation. By one more person... sheesh

Motivation to what? Block your Twitter account?

Ashlynn Yennie (@ashlynnyennie)
I was told by my agent I dont look like a girl who drinks beer but ad agencies disagree...These are my problems right now

Pretty charmed life. Jay-Z has way more problems than that.

Alyssa Russell (@alyssarussell)
This could be the longest time I've ever waited for makeup

She means she's in the makeup chair on a set because she is an actress on a thing, y'all.

Ricky Williams (@RickyWilliams)
I just received a text that I was the top story on NFL.com. I'm trying to stay out of the news.

Then stop tweetin' about it. You're just making us wanna go to the site you're trying to stay off of. Unless you secretly LIKE the attention...

Marcus Brigstocke (@marcusbrig)
According to Amazon I am both a 'mover' + a 'shaker'...

They must have seen me dancing. They missed off grinder, winder, voguer + bogeler.

This was quite the long walk! Not worth it!

Jay Bilas (@JayBilas)
Jeff Van Gundy hasn't seen Pulp Fiction. But, he knew White Shadow episode I was in, circa 1979, line by line. Guy needs to get out more.

"Get out more"? So he can go see Pulp Fiction?

Stephen Mangan (@StephenMangan)
Just filmed the first scene of my new job. Always a relief. Harder to fire me now.

Your new job wouldn't happen to be "actor," would it?

Moe (@Monimus)
I got 99 problems, but fucking ridiculous women that sleep with you then tell you they're dating someone is one.

Sounds more like that other guy's problem.

Al Yankovic (@alyankovic)
Common review for #Alpocalypse: "It's really good,
but not nearly as great as (whichever Weird Al record I
listened to when I was 12)"

*Hey, at least they liked you at one time, Al. Wait, lemme Weird Al that
up: Hey, at.. YEAST... they HIKED... you at one... SLIME?
I'm not so good at this.*

Jay Mohr (@jaymohr37)
If u look at my career in reverse, I'm doing amazing.
Humble start in podcast +stand up-crecendo with Jen
Aniston rom-com +Tom Cruise movie.

You left out Gary Unmarried (guess it would hurt the joke)!

Janko Tipsarevic (@TipsarevicJanko)
Cant't believe I am in the gym on my holidays...Whats
wrong with me??...

*Uh, you care too much about your physical appearance or are over-
compensating for some other shit?*

Kyle (@DumbNOTDeaf)
Someone just referred to me & said that I have fans.

If people are actually 'Fans' of me that's a sign of the apocalypse. May God have mercy

Who said that?

derek webb (@derekwebb)
sometimes i wonder if the reason i come off as insightful is because I'm a really good liar

Can't help ya there, but I can say that the reason you come off as annoying is because of this statement.

BNycesty (@MissRedboneUSA)
#dearyoungself get your royalties for the song u recorded at laface records when u were 17…#YOUBASTARDS

Dear older self, quit humblebragging about your achievements from your younger days.

Kirbie (@kirbiej)
Never can watch Zefron kiss Nikki Blonsky. Or anyone for that matter. I think it's because he looks too much like my ex from high school

How often are you in jeopardy of watching Zac Efron kiss people?
Probably not that often, right?

🐷 🐷 🐷

Ashley (@YeahImAshley)
None of these motherfucking dildos fit.

This one is one of my favorites ever. A tight vagina humblebrag.
Now I've seen everything. Though, I suppose there is an off-chance
she meant none of them were big enough, in which case I take it back
and convey my sympathies.

Humblebrags in Academy Awards Acceptance Speeches

Twitter is clearly the best online receptacle for humble-brags; however, there is no place where real-life humblebrags are more on display than awards show acceptance speeches. And the Academy Awards is basically the Super bowl of this form of humblebragging. One of my least favorite ones that people constantly do is the: "I didn't expect to win, so I didn't prepare a speech." For real?? You didn't prepare a speech? You are one of six people on the entire planet who is up for the award and you didn't think you maybe had an outside chance of winning? Maybe just think about what you would say, like, for a minute. Just a minute of your day. During your morning piss, how about you maybe bat around a couple of ideas so you don't go up there and just pant for thirty straight seconds?

I guess I can't totally blame them. The nature of an acceptance speech is humble by design. It's always awkward taking a compliment. At an awards show, the world just told someone that they are the best at something, and they have to take that compliment in a graceful way, in front of millions of viewers. I am sure I would be annoying, too. But until someone changes the game on how to accept an award in a tolerable manner, I gotta call some of these people out...

(Note: For the sake of not boring you, I have taken short excerpts from the following speeches. I didn't think you'd care about reading the names of Colin Firth's thirty lawyers.)

David Bretherton, Film Editing, *Cabaret*, March 27, 1973
"I only wish tonight that my mouth was...as talented as my hands so I could thank you all very much."

Too bad there's no Oscar for tooting your own horn, huh?

Jack Nicholson, Best Actor, One *Flew Over the Cuckoo's Nest*, March 29, 1976
"Well, I guess this proves there are as many nuts in the Academy as anywhere else....And speaking of a percentage, last but not least, my agent, who about ten years ago advised me that I had no business being an actor. Thank you."

He was so unsure of himself back then. Where did Jack Nicholson get all of his confidence since 1976? Oh, right: pills, I'm guessing. Lots and lots of pills.

Bo Goldman, Best Adapted Screenplay, One *Flew Over the Cuckoo's Nest*, March 29, 1976

"I loved writing this movie and it seems redundant to me to receive an award when the only award I ever wanted was a chance to write a script like this."

You can't trick me with your verbal gymnastics and grammatical loopty-loops! This was a humblebrag!

Mark Johnson, Producer, Best Picture, *Rain Man*,
March 29, 1989
"I've been told for the past five weeks that maybe I should prepare for this, and I can't be prepared for this moment."

Well, you could have. You know . . . , by writing a speech and stuff.

Akira Kurosawa, Honorary Award, March 26, 1990
"I am very deeply honored to receive such a wonderful prize, but I have to ask whether I really deserve it. I'm a little worried, because I don't feel that I understand cinema yet. I really don't feel that I have yet grasped the essence of cinema. Cinema is a marvelous thing, but to grasp its true essence is very, very difficult. But what I promise you is that from now on I will work as hard as I can at making movies and maybe by following this path I will achieve an understanding of the true essence of cinema and earn this award."

I don't think you've grasped the true essence of chillin' out. Relax, Kurosawa.

Bruce Springsteen, Best Original Song, *Philadelphia*, March 21, 1994
"Thank you. Gee, this is the first song I ever wrote for a motion picture, so I guess it's all downhill from here."

You're gonna be OOOOHKAY, Boss.

Frances McDormand, Best Actress, *Fargo*, March 24, 1997
"It is impossible to maintain one's composure in this situation. What am I doing here?"

Another case of an actor not understanding that sometimes if you act, you get awards for it. Why is this such a complicated concept to get a handle on??

Keiko Ibi, Best Documentary Short Subject, *The Personals: Improvisations on Romance in the Golden Years*, March 21, 1999
"Thank you. Who would have thought a girl from Japan can make a movie about Jewish senior citizens and actually receive this award?"

Honestly, not me. But this still qualifies as a humblebrag.

James Coburn, Best Supporting Actor, *Affliction*, March 21, 1999
"My my my. Wow. You know, I've been around here—I've been working and doing this work for like over half my life. And I finally got one right, I guess."

Never saw it.

Roberto Benigni, Best Actor, *Life Is Beautiful*,
March 21, 1999
"Thank you!....really I don't deserve this, but I hope
to win some other Oscars! Thank you! Thank you very
much! Thank you!"

*I vividly remember watching this speech. I hadn't seen his movie yet.
I just remember a strange little Italian man shouting about wanting to
have sex with everyone in the room. And it was adorable. Truly a classic speech. But he slipped this in at the end, so I gotta put him on blast!*

*You don't think you deserve it, but you want MORE Oscars?
Something doesn't add up, Benigni...*

Stephen Gaghan, Best Adapted Screenplay, *Traffic*,
March 25, 2001
"If I made up a story where someone like me would find
himself somewhere like this, nobody would believe it.
Nobody here...And most importantly, four years ago a lot
of people reached out their hands to me and helped me
out, and this is for you, guys. Thanks."

*I don't know this guy's story, but a screenwriter writing a screenplay
and then receiving an award for said screenplay is highly within the
realm of believability. If he won a Cy Young Award in 2001, I
would have been all, "Whaaaaaat?!!!!"*

Denzel Washington, Best Actor, *Training Day*,
March 24, 2002
"Forty years I've been chasing Sidney [Poitier], they
finally give it to me, what'd they do? They give it to him

the same night. I'll always be chasing you, Sidney.
I'll always be following in your footsteps.
"You know, when I was in college first starting out as
an actor, they asked each one of us what we wanted to
do. I said I want to be the best actor in the world. All the
students in the classroom looked at me like I was a nut.
Life has taught me to just try and be the best that I can
be, and I thank the Academy for saying to me that on this
given night I was the best that I could be."

*I actually enjoy both of these sentiments. Don't get me wrong;
they're both humblebrags, but they're pretty inoffensive and jovial.
Well done, Denzel.*

Randy Newman, Best Original Song, *Monsters, Inc.,*
March 24, 2002
"Thank you. I don't want your pity…I have nothing, I'm
absolutely astounded that I've won for this, though the
picture deserves recognition."

*Right, but this award is for the music category. Best Animated Fea-
ture is a whole separate thing. They'll get recognized there. Don't
worry about it, Randy. Relax. Enjoy.*

Ronald Harwood, Best Adapted Screenplay, *The Pianist,*
March 23, 2003
"When I was last here twenty years ago—I'm not making a
habit of it, don't worry—Shirley MacLaine got Best Actress.
And when she got the statue she said, 'I deserve this.'
Well, I wish I could say that, but I can't. Roman Polanski

deserves this. He's a great director and a wonderful colleague. And I want to thank him and, of course, you for this splendid honor. Thank you very much indeed."

Sorry you only get nominated for an Oscar once every twenty years. That sucks, man. Also, great idea to say the guy who molested a child deserves an award more than you. Bold move!

Adrien Brody, Best Actor, *The Pianist*, March 23, 2003
"Oh my God. Thank you. Thank you, really. Oh my goodness. It doesn't come out in slow motion, but it doesn't really ring a bell—the name. I didn't know my name when you said that. This Adrien? Okay."

Of course they mean you, ya' big goof!

"...There comes a time in life when everything seems to make sense and this is not one of those times."

What doesn't make sense? Ya' won an Oscar, ya' big goof!

"And if it weren't for the insomnia and those sudden panic attacks, this has been an amazing, amazing journey."

Gotta get up on that Ambien and Xanax, ya' big goof!

Brad Bird, Best Animated Feature, *The Incredibles*, February 27, 2005

"Thank you so much. I don't know what's more frightening, being watched by millions of people, or the hundreds of people that are going to be annoyed with me tomorrow for not mentioning them tonight."

Pixar-brag.

Hilary Swank, Best Actress, *Million Dollar Baby*, February 27, 2005
"I don't know what I did in this life to deserve all this. I'm just a girl from a trailer park who had a dream. I never thought this would ever happen, let alone be nominated. And a working actor, for that matter. And now, this."

There's roughly four humblebrags in this one paragraph, and this is only part of her speech.

George Clooney, Best Actor, *Syriana*, March 5, 2006
"Wow. Wow. All right, so I'm not winning Director. It's a funny thing about winning an Academy Award, this will always be sort of synonymous with your name from here on in. It will be: Oscar winner George Clooney, Sexiest Man Alive 1997, Batman, died today in a freak accident....
"Listen, I don't quite know how you compare art. You look at these performances this year, of these actors, and unless we all did the same role—everybody put on a bat suit, we'll all try that—unless we all did the same role, I don't know how you compare it. They are stellar

performances and wonderful work, and I'm honored, truly honored to be up here."

Clooney employs some masterful humblebragging here. He references his turn as Batman in one of the worst movies ever made, multiple times in fact. Then he makes fun of the fact that he won Sexiest Man Alive nine years ago. Then he makes a grandiose postulation about not knowing how one "compares art."

Kids, take note. THIS is how you humblebrag.

Martin Scorsese, Best Director, *The Departed,*
February 25, 2007
"Thank you. Thank you. Thank you. Thank you. Thank you. Rick! Thank you. Thank you. Thank you. Please, please. Thank you. Thank you. Could you double-check the envelope?"

Never was a humblebrag more warranted than this moment, if you ask me. Scorsese is one of the greatest directors of all time and was snubbed for years by the Academy. It would have been weird if he DIDN'T say some sort of self-effacing comment. That being said, gotta include him in this book.

Also, who is Rick? He just yells "Rick" at some point.

Kate Winslet, Best Actress, *The Reader,* February 22, 2009
"I want to acknowledge my fellow nominees, these goddesses. I think we all can't believe we're in a category with Meryl Streep at all. I'm sorry, Meryl, but you have to just suck that up!"

Now, this was a very interesting maneuver on the part of Kate Winslet. She managed to humblebrag for four other people. Don't drag them into this, Winslet. Let them lose gracefully.

Sean Penn, Best Actor, *Milk*, February 22, 2009
"Thank you. Thank you. You commie, homo-loving
sons-of-guns! I did not expect this, but I, and I want
it to be very clear that I do know how hard I make
it to appreciate me, often. But I am touched by the
appreciation and I hoped for it enough that I did want
to scribble down so I had the names, in case you were
commie, homo-loving sons-of-guns."

Didn't expect it, but you wrote down some names to thank? Sounds like someone expected it a little bit...

Sandra Bullock, Best Actress, *The Blind Side*,
March 7, 2010
"Did I really earn this or did I just wear you all down?"

Wear them down? What else did you want it for? Speed? But seriously, you're charming and I love you.

Pete Docter, Best Animated Feature, *Up*, March 7, 2010,
"Boy, never did I dream that making a flip book out of my
third grade math book would lead to this. Boy."

THAT'S how you got a job at Pixar?! (Bonus to him on this one for using "boy" twice. It's very Jimmy Stewart of him and it amps up the humble three-fold.)

Colin Firth, Best Actor, *The King's Speech*,
February 27, 2011
"I have a feeling my career has just peaked. My deepest
thanks to the Academy. I'm afraid I have to warn you
that I'm experiencing stirrings, somewhere in the upper
abdominals, which are threatening to form themselves
into dance moves which, joyous as they may be for me,
it would be extremely problematic if they make it to my
legs before I get offstage. So I'm going to do my best to be
brief with my gratitude.

Whoa, whoa, whoa. Just say you feel like dancing. Actually wait,
just say "thank you."

Melissa Leo, Best Supporting Actress, *The Fighter*,
February 27, 2011
"Oh my, oh my God. Oh wow really, really, really, really,
really, truly wow. I know there's a lot of people that said
a lotta real real nice things to me for several months now,
but I'm just shaking in my boots here."

I didn't take any liberties with how many times she said "oh my" or
"wow" or "really." That is truly how many times she said "oh my,"
"wow," and "really."

Christian Bale, Best Supporting Actor, *The Fighter*,
February 27, 2011
"Bloody hell. Wow. What a roomful of talented and
inspirational people and what the hell am I doing here in
the midst of you?"

Hey man, we all listened to that outburst you had on set. We know
you think you're a very good and serious actor. Jig is up!

Natalie Portman Best Actress, *Black Swan,*
February 27, 2011
"Thank you so much to the Academy...this is insane and
I truly sincerely wish that the prize tonight was to get to
work with my fellow nominees. I'm so in awe of you."

Will you settle for just the Oscar? Cool?

Now What?

So now you know what a humblebrag is. Unfortunately, now you can't un-know it. You will hear it everywhere you go; from your dentist to your dad to your lover and so on. You can see the matrix. Now, the choice is up to you if you want to call it out or not. Bear in mind that calling people out on humblebragging in your daily life will eventually make everyone so uneasy around you they will stop talking to you altogether. No one likes to be around cops and the same goes for word cops. But you also can't stand idly by. It's a problem that only seems to be getting worse.

As we learned in the Humblebrags from Throughout History chapter, it's a very longstanding social occurrence, but with the advent of social media, humblebragging is clearly at an all-time high. And as technology progresses, so will humblebragging probably. Eventually we will be able to communicate humblebrags in unimaginable ways, perhaps merely with our minds! I'm just hoping that when the robots inevitably form a consciousness and take over the planet, they won't also co-opt this human trend. Can you imagine what future robot humblebrags would be like? "I wish my bi-fractal radon-phaser wasn't so irridescent. Serves me right for spending five million zortocks on it!" It's like, we get it, robot, you have a lot of zortocks!

Okay, I have gotten grossly off topic. The point is, I'm not saying everyone should just stop humblebragging entirely (I would like to get to do another volume of this book, after-all). Be proud of your acheivements! I'm proud of you. Great job. All of you. I love how much money you just made on the big deal. Sweet new car, man! Of course guys on the bus are hitting on you; you're gorgeous, baby.

Go out there and humblebrag to your heart's content. Just maybe don't do it so often and so publicly? Maybe consider only doing it to your close friends and relatives, who know without a doubt that you mean well. Because, I promise you, it kinda just bums everyone else out.

Acknowledgments

I thought about doing a "funny" acknowledgment section, but would a little sincerity kill me? No, it wouldn't. Also, I had to write a lot of fucking jokes for this thing and it's like midnight the night before this is due and I'm burned out, so I'm just gonna do real thank-yous.

I would like to thank Mom, Dad, Steph, and Ganny. (My family is genuinely hilarious, not just for family. They genuinely are good at jokes and laughing.) Thanks to my fantastic editor, Ben Greenberg, and Grand Central Publishing. Josh Lieberman, Richard Abate, Dave Becky, Tom Lassally and everyone at 3Arts, Bill Zotti, Grant Kessman, Greg Cavic, Rachel Rusch, Michael Kives, Pam Klier, and CAA. Also thank you, Jared Levine.

Thank you to Taal Douadi for the research and the friendship, the *Parks and Recreation* writing staff (Mike "Mark" Schur, Dan, Alan, Davis, Dipps, Chels, Yeeshy, Norm, Scully, Kapnek, Spives, Axler, Greg, DP, B. Rowe, and Greg L. Can you believe this, you guys?), the *Parks and Rec* cast, Armen Weitzman (Karf?), Mitch (Sports), Matty Marcus, Paul Rust and Mike Cassady (2 goji's), Lesley Arfin, Jim and Kyle, Sam and Natalia, Noah, Gabe, Joe, Levy, Taylor,

Singer, Nick Thorburn, Neil Campbell, Susan and the UCB Theatre, Bday Boys, AKFD, Guys' Night, Sarah Silverman for everything ever, Dan Sterling, Jon Schroeder, Rob Schrab, Bill Simmons, Dan Fierman, Grantland, Danny, Jody, Brandon, Reilly, Alex, and Rough House, Louis CK, Scott, Kulap, Rocky, Eli Bush, Scott Rudin, and Tim Riggins.

A special huge thanks to everyone who follows **@humblebrag** and to anyone who has ever sent in a humblebrag to be retweeted—you shall remain anonymous and I remain grateful.

All of my ex-girlfriends. And Phish!

Sorry to anyone I forgot, but you just didn't play that big of a role in this book. Try to step it up for volume two.

Sources

Humblebrags from Throughout History

Page 91: "With fame I become more and more stupid"; Helen Dukas, and Banesh Hoffman, eds. *Albert Einstein: The Human Side. New Glimpses from His Archives.* Princeton: Princeton University Press, 1979.

Page 92: "Do not worry about your difficulties in mathematics; I can assure you that mine are still greater"; *Albert Einstein: The Human Side. New Glimpses from His Archives.*

Page 92: "The news gang are forever riding me" and "You'd think I had unlimited power and a swell pocketbook"; from an interview with Cornelius Vanderbilt Jr.; *Liberty*, October 17, 1931.

Page 93: "I have not succeeded"; from an interview with Hayden Church; *Liberty*, 7 February 1931.

Pages 94 and 95: "[God] gave me this extraordinary wife" and "Complete ugliness, utter ugliness"; interview by Oriana Fallaci, 1964, published in *The Egotists: Sixteen Amazing Interviews*, 1968.

Page 95: "I don't need much more money"; Steve Miller. "Johnny Ramone: Rebel in a Rebel's World." *The Washington Times*, March 11, 2004.

Page 96: "The thrill and embarrassment of becoming international pop stars"; Details magazine, 1993.

Page 96: "I may not be well read, but when I do read, I read well"; Journals by Kurt Cobain, Riverhead Publishing, 2002.

Page 96: "I spent all of my life trying to stay away from sports"; http://www.livenirvana.com/tourhistory/index.html.

Page 96: "I can't play [guitar] like Segovia"; *Fender Frontline,* Fall 1994.

Page 96: "A lot of people are just really confused by me"; Frank Broughton. *Time Out Interviews 1968–1998.* London: Penguin Putnam, 1998.

Page 97: "I mean, how do you explain the fact—everybody in the United States knows me"; Paul Krassner. *Impolite Interviews.* New York: Seven Stories Press, 1999.

Page 98: "The Who are rapidly becoming a circus act"; Frank Broughton, *Time Out Interviews 1968–1998.* London: Penguin Putnam, 1998.